World Wide Waste

How digital is killing our planet—
and what we can do about it

About the author

Gerry McGovern has been working on Web content and data issues since 1994. A highly regarded speaker, he has spoken on such issues around 40 countries. He has written seven other books on digital content.

Gerry developed Top Tasks, a research method to understand what truly matters to customers. Top Tasks has been used by organizations such as Microsoft, Cisco, NetApp, Toyota, World Health Organization, IBM, the European Union, US, UK, Dutch, Canadian, Norwegian, and Irish governments.

The Irish Times has described him as one of five visionaries who have had a major impact on the development of the Web. He has appeared on BBC, CNN and CNBC television, partaken in various radio shows, and featured in numerous print media publications. He is the founder and CEO of Customer Carewords.

@gerrymcgovern
gerry@gerrymcgovern.com
www.gerrymcgovern.com

World Wide Waste

How digital is killing our planet—
and what we can do about it

Gerry McGovern

Silver Beach Publishing
2020

First edition 2020

ISBN 978-1-9164446-2-1

Silver Beach Publishing
Silver Beach
Gormanston
Meath
Ireland
K32 YN40

www.gerrymcgovern.com

Cover Design: Lisa Coffey
Layout & editing: Simon Coury
Editing: Rosilda Moreira Alves McGovern

Contents

Acknowledgements

Thanks to Rosilda, my inspiring and beautiful wife. She started me on this path. Educated me on the need to consider and care for the environment. Thanks to Greta Thunberg and the millions of young and old environmentalists. What an education I have received from the young! How they have led in an era of toxic older "leaders."

Thanks to Patrick O'Beirne, a numbers wizard, who gave invaluable advice and checked up on the many calculations throughout the book. Daniel Marchewka also did some great technical analysis and calculations. Simon Coury did excellent editing and laid out the manuscript. Lisa Coffey did her usual high-quality cover design. Thanks to Alastair Somerville for suggesting the book title and Gerry Scullion for the subtitle.

I got important feedback on various drafts from Geoff Simpson, Todd Libby, Brandon McNeely, Marghretta McBean, Abbe Winter, Eva Sanagustin, Liam Nugent, Toon Lowette, Ernst Décsey, Jason Dinsdale, Jonathan Rath, Karl Turner, Jeroen Schalk, Conxa Rodà de Llanza, Ciara Pidgeon, Paul Kelly, Melissa Richardson.

Who is this book for?

This book is primarily for digital professionals, whether involved in management, code, content or design. It is also more focused on organizations and the behavior than occurs within them. It should be of interest to environmental champions who are looking for more actions to take to care of the Earth.

The basic principles that will be explored throughout the book, however, can apply to our personal lives, and should be of interest to a general reader, though they may find a couple of chapters somewhat technical.

The community of digital professionals is one I've been privileged to be a part of for 25 years. I've always felt that it was generally an idealistic group of people, drawn to an emerging and exciting space, who want to play their part in creating a better world, and certainly don't want to be part of a process that is killing the planet. I think we have been blind to the dark side of digital, to its hidden energy costs, to its wasteful habits. I know I certainly have.

I have spent most of my career championing user/customer experience. I have constantly talked about the need for being customer-centric. I now believe we must be, first and foremost, Earth-centric. We have raised humans above nature for too long.

We have long since discovered that the Earth is not the center of the universe, but it is the center of our universe. We must focus on and design for Earth Experience because right now we are on an accelerated path of destruction, and digital is a primary accelerant.

Introduction: Why digital is killing our planet

Digital is physical

Digital is physical. Every byte is supported by an atom. Every single action in digital costs the Earth energy. Turn the electricity off and you turn digital off. Digital is demanding an increasing share of the Earth's energy and resources and is a major contributor to the generation of toxic trash, to a culture of disposability, convenience and the most wasteful behavior ever seen in human history.

Used wisely, digital could be saving our planet, making things more productive and efficient, and more environmentally friendly, while improving living standards. Right now, however, digital is killing our planet. It is helping make the rich the super-rich, the middle class the working class, and the working class the working poor.

The climate is warming, reaching dangerous levels at abnormal speeds. "It is extremely likely that human influence has been the dominant cause of the observed warming since the mid-20th century," the Intergovernmental Panel on Climate Change has stated. "These findings have been recognized by the national science academies of the major industrialized nations and are not disputed by any scientific body of national or international standing," Wikipedia has confirmed.

We are using resources at unsustainable levels and we are creating massive quantities of useless and often dangerous waste. It's all speeding up at a frenetic pace. In the last 50 years, humans have been wasting the Earth at unprecedented levels. In the last 50 years, digital technology has grown at unprecedented levels.

For us lucky enough to be employed in digital it has been boom time. In my home country, Ireland, digital has turned parts of the Emerald Isle into the Silicon Isle. In Dublin, the average annual pay packet of a Facebook employee in 2017 was €154,000, according to the Irish Times, with the average Irish full-time salary being €46,000. Yet while the tech elite thrive, much of the rest of society struggles.

I was lucky enough to catch the Internet wave back around 1994. It was incredibly exciting and financially rewarding. It seemed obvious to me that digital was a good thing for our society and economy. When more people started talking about global warming in the early 2000s, I felt lucky to be involved in a sector that I believed was inherently environmentally friendly. Becoming more digital seemed like the answer to global warming. Our physical activities were destroying the planet, but our digital activities would help save it. That's what I believed.

I had some nagging doubts, though. Since the late Nineties, I have worked on a lot of intranets and internal systems. Peering inside a typical organization at their IT infrastructure was like going on an archaeological dig. The external "branding" may have made the organization look modern but the internal IT systems had that ancient feeling to them, riven with complexity and appallingly designed; usability close to zero.

In organization after organization I was told by employees that it was really hard to find anything on the intranet. It took them literally years to understand how arcane systems worked and where everything was, and they could only do that by constantly asking questions of more experienced employees. As time went by, things weren't improving. As I was writing this book, I talked to a developer at one of the world's largest IT consultancies. Their own intranet was a joke, a nightmare, he told me. This isn't the promise of IT. Software isn't supposed to suck this much.

I began to wonder whether we had too much digital "planned obsolescence" "innovation" and not enough social and organizational innovation. Had digital become a creature trained to eat itself, waste itself, replace itself as quickly as possible so as to maximize short-term growth?

Do we have too much software and hardware, and too little quality design, too little quality thinking? Too little time to do the right thing in an age of digital gadgets and services promising to save us time?

Digital puts you on speed. Digital is a stressor. You can move 50,000 words in digital around the world in seconds. Moving a 50,000-word book is going to require a lot more effort and time. Because we can do things much faster in digital, we do. Its nature calls us to speed up. Left in its natural state, digital gets faster and faster. Nearly all the digital projects I was involved with were hungry for the low-hanging fruit, the quick wins. "We know this is the right way to do it, but we don't have time," was a recurrent mantra. We don't have time to do it right. We only have time to do it wrong.

In the last 50 years, while there has been a huge investment in information technology, productivity and return on assets have been poor. "You can see the computer age everywhere but in the productivity statistics," Nobel laureate Robert Solow stated in 1987. There was a positive productivity uptake during the mid-Nineties but since the Great Recession, that has fallen away severely. Between 2010 and 2020, productivity growth in the UK, for example, was a truly miserable 0.3%, according to the Royal Statistical Society. "The UK has just had its worst decade for productivity growth since the early 1800s," Harriet Grant wrote for The Guardian in 2019. Since the 1800s?

The tech evangelists have been making the argument that we should expect a delay from when a new technology is launched to when the society and economy fully understands how to get the best out of it. Maybe. They've been making that argument for decades now. A much deeper issue than productivity is general societal prosperity. Artificial intelligence promises to eliminate not just working-class jobs but also many middle-class ones. Digital has and will continue to deliver inordinate rewards for a tiny elite, while taking the jobs of millions and turning millions of others into low paid "gig economy" serfs. Digital concentrates power. Digital concentrates wealth.

Correlation is not causation. Just because massive investments in digital technology are correlated with a rapid increase in global warming, rapid growth in natural resource depletion, huge increases in waste production, poor productivity, and a decline in the middle class in the very economies who have embraced digital the most, it does not mean that digital caused all these things.

Digital could be an innocent bystander to historical events outside its control or ability to influence. Which is a bit worrying, isn't it? I totally bought into this whole Digital Revolution thing that kicked off in the mid-Nineties with the advent of the World Wide Web. If we're saying that there's no causation here, are we also saying that Facebook, Apple, Amazon, and Google (FANG) don't matter that much to the big picture? That FANG has had no real impact—either positive or negative—on global warming, productivity and the decline of the middle class? That the Web itself is neither here nor there when it comes to the lives of ordinary people? That all this Digital Revolution stuff is just tech candy? That's a hard sell, isn't it?

Digital is no innocent bystander. Digital matters. Digital is shaping our lives. Digital is shaping our planet. Digital is an accelerant and a concentrator. Right now, it is accelerating bad behavior and concentrating wealth. Digital puts the foot to the pedal and shunts us forward at a speed we are currently not capable of coping with. Beyond certain points, speed becomes dangerous and highly wasteful. We are racing into the future with no seat belt.

Earth Overshoot Day marks the date when we have used more natural resources than the Earth can regenerate in a given year. In 2019, it was July 29. It is the "advanced" digital economies that are doing by far the most overshooting. In the United States, 2019 Overshoot Day arrived on March 15, in Canada on March 16, in Denmark on March 29, in Sweden on April 3, in Finland on April 6. At the other end of the calendar, in Indonesia Overshoot Day didn't arrive until December 18, in Ecuador on December 14, in Iraq on December 7. Think of what would happen to the Earth if every country became an "advanced" digital nation? Whether global warming is happening or not, the way we live in the "advanced" digital world is not sustainable.

Every year, Overshoot Day gets earlier. When the 1970s started, it was close to January 1, so we were in a type of balance, with the Earth renewing at the same pace as we were using up resources. As you'll see throughout this book, in the last 40–50 years we've gone into hyperdrive, using up everything at a pace never before seen in human history.

Useless waste

Up to 90% of what we take from the Earth and make into digital stuff, quickly ends up as waste, much of it useless, toxic and dangerous. Digital is the most ravenous and fastest growing child in a mob of production hunting down natural resources. According to the 2019 International Resource Panel report:

- The use of natural resources has more than tripled since 1970 and continues to grow.
- From 2000 to 2015, the climate change and health impacts from extraction and production of metals doubled.
- 90% of biodiversity loss and water stress are caused by resource extraction and processing.

Consumption is ramping up at a speed never before experienced in human history. China consumed 6.6 gigatons of cement between 2011 and 2013. That's more cement than the US consumed during the entire 20th century, Forbes reported. "The world has almost doubled its energy consumption since 1980," Bloomberg reported in 2019.

It is hard to even imagine how wasteful we are as a species. The more research I did for this book, the more shocked I became. Huge quantities of products never even get bought and end up as waste. The stuff we buy, a great deal of it we barely even use—it ends up as waste. We hardly recycle. Most stuff goes straight to the dump or into the ocean. Humans are wasters.

Digital encourages extreme waste and an extreme waste mindset. I will focus throughout this book on how 90% of what we do in digital is either useless waste to begin with or else quickly ends up in a data dump or a physical dump. 90%. It's one thing to deplete natural resources in order to create useful things, things that we need to live, to eat, to keep warm, to get around in, to be entertained with. To dig up the Earth in order to create a giant dump of unnecessary crap, of half-baked products and services, of gadgets that meet nothing but a passing whim, to leave YouTube streaming in an empty room on a large screen, to back up files that have absolutely no useful function, that sort of behavior should make us feel ashamed.

"72% of the global ice-free land surface is dedicated to supporting humans," according to Mark Lynas writing for CNN in 2019. There are at least five million species and possibly many more, according to research by the University of Sydney, but between a quarter and a third of the entire output of the world's plants is consumed by the human species.

In the last 40 years, there has been a 60% decline in the population sizes of mammals, birds, fish, reptiles, and amphibians, according to the World Wildlife Fund. "More than half of all insects may have disappeared since 1970," the World Economic Forum reported in 2020. The UN has described the situation as "unprecedented" and "accelerating." Digital rises, nature declines.

I still believe that, properly used, digital can help us conserve this beautiful planet. It is digital that is helping us analyze the vast amount of data on climate. It is digital that allows us to make reasonably accurate predictions. Digital can help us plan better and work more efficiently, thus saving energy and resources. Digital has massive positive potential.

Thinking in trees

There are about three trillion trees in the world, according research by Thomas Crowther, a professor at Yale. Since the beginning of human civilization, the global number of trees has fallen by about 46%. We lose 15 billion trees a year, according to Time magazine, and plant five billion, according to Tentree, giving us a net loss of 10 billion.

Trees breathe carbon dioxide and exhale oxygen, which makes them an ideal part of the solution to climate change. A part. The scientific consensus is that it is not possible to plant nearly enough trees to even come close to combating global warming. We need to plant ideas and take action even faster. Ideas that focus on consuming less and conserving more.

Trees can absorb anything from 6 kg to 22 kg of CO_2 per year. "The average Pine tree absorbs about 10 kilograms of CO_2 per year," GoTreeQuotes states. For simplicity purposes, I will use a figure of 10 kg in my calculations throughout the rest of the book.

It's not that simple, though. It never is. Almost all trees both emit and absorb methane, a gas that, while it lasts in the atmosphere for a lot less time than CO_2, is estimated to be 30 times more polluting. In tropical rainforests, in particular, trees can emit substantially more methane than they absorb. However, "In the wider world of climate change, their benefits are almost always much greater," researcher Sunitha Pangala told YaleEnvironment360. "Even for an individual tree, the methane element usually turns out to be quite small compared to carbon storage." Trees, of course, have many other benefits, as journalist Fred Pearce points out: "They recycle moisture, create shade, stimulate cloud formation, protect biodiversity, and cleanse the air."

It was only relatively recently that Sunitha Pangala's research helped identify the methane impact of trees, and she did it with the support of digital technology. Digital can help us understand our world much better. It can give us the information that can help us to optimize our environment, to target where the waste comes from, and to promote activities that conserve. Perhaps there are certain types of tree that produce less methane? Digital can help us find out. But we must want to do this. We must want to conserve. We must want to not waste.

We need to plant more trees. Again, here's where technology can help. Drones can plant trees 150 times faster than traditional methods and with tremendous accuracy, reaching areas that are inaccessible to humans. They're also cheaper.

This is not a book about digital's amazing potential. It is a book about why we have not nearly realized that potential, how we are in fact currently using it in ways that are destructive to societal wellbeing and the wellbeing of the planet. I'm going to suggest actions that we can take to take control of digital so that we use it for more positive purposes.

One of the most difficult challenges with digital is to truly grasp what it is, its form, its impact on the physical world. I want to help give you a feel for digital. Throughout the book, I'm going to analyze how many trees would need to be planted to offset a particular digital activity. For example:

- 1.6 billion trees would have to be planted to offset the pollution caused by email spam.
- 1.5 billion trees would need to be planted to deal with annual e-commerce returns in the US alone.
- 231 million trees would need to be planted to deal with the pollution caused as a result of the data US citizens consumed in a 2019.
- 16 million trees would need to be planted to offset the pollution caused by the estimated 1.9 trillion yearly searches on Google.

Print or digital?

When I started off writing this book my idea was that it should only be available in a digital format because that would be much more environmentally friendly than a print version. I wanted to show that, under the right circumstances, digital was clearly better for the environment. As I did my research, I found that it was not as simple as I had first thought.

Digital creates a sort of mirage when it comes to environmental friendliness. It can feel better for the environment to read something on a screen than to pick up a physical book. A digital book feels "lighter" than a physical book. All is not what it seems. The weight of digital is displaced from the book itself to the device upon which you read it, and from the device to the data center and the network that stores and delivers the book.

Increasingly, your behavior as you read the book is being analyzed. That costs energy. There is always a weight to digital, always a cost to the Earth. Too often it is a hidden weight and a hidden cost.

When we look out across a physical landscape, we can generally get a sense of it. It's not so easy with digital. Our senses were not designed for digital interactions. We can be easily fooled. We need to train ourselves better to understand the true nature of digital, the true impact of digital on ourselves and on the Earth, as well as its true potential to make the environment better. We can do this. It will take time and effort.

According to a 2010 New York Times analysis, one e-reader required 50 times the minerals and 40 times the amount of water to manufacture than a print book. You'd need to read more than 100 books on an e-reader before it would have a lower pollution impact than reading the equivalent number of print books. A 2009 analysis by Clean Tech consultancy had a much lower figure, estimating that you'd only need to read about 23 books on an e-reader before it would be a better choice for the environment.

In 2016, Pew Research reported that a typical US citizen reads about four books a year. That would mean that an average person would need to hold on to their e-reader anywhere from six to 25 years for it to become the environmentally friendly choice.

Another thing that tends to happen in digital—particularly in the "free" model—is download without consumption. Richard Lea, writing for The Guardian in 2015, reported on studies of e-book reading that showed that 60% of e-books bought were never opened. The completion rates for those that were started could be as low as 20%. Not surprisingly, one study by e-book maker Kobo found that the more people paid for a book, they more likely they were to read it. Waste flows from the free mindset.

70% to 90% of the total pollution caused by a digital device is caused during its manufacture. This is a relatively new phenomenon, as traditional manufactured electrical/petrol-based products tend to cause most of their pollution during their lifetime of use. What this means is that the moment you buy an e-reader you acquire something that has already caused very significant pollution. It needs to be used a lot before it is "better" for the environment than reading in print.

Of course, using something digital does cause some pollution. There is the cost of downloading the content and there is the cost of processing and reading it. If the content is "free" then these costs can be substantial because digital advertising, which underpins the free model, is highly toxic and environmentally damaging.

A 2009 study from the Swedish KTH Center for Sustainable Communications found that if you read news for about 10 minutes a day, then digital was a more environmentally friendly option. However, if you read news for more than 30 minutes a day, a print newspaper was the best option. A 2019 study of music streaming by the University of Glasgow and the University of Oslo found that if you listened to a particular song a lot, it would be better to play that song from a CD or have it stored on your local hard drive, rather than constantly streaming it.

Luckily, books are generally not advertising dependent, so the impact of a particular book is down to its file size. The things that influence digital file size include:

- The number of images, charts and tables used and the formats they are saved in.
- Whether the book is full color or black and white.
- The number of pages.
- The type of font being used. If it is a standard font, the impact will be low. If it is a custom font the impact will be higher.
- The number of words have relatively little impact on file size because text itself is by far the most environmentally friendly form of communication.

In 2018, I published Top Tasks. It was almost 42,000 words. It was in black and white except for a simple two-color cover. This book, World Wide Waste, is 51,000 words. It's in black and white, including cover.

Top Tasks had quite a few tables and webpage screengrabs. Its epub file size was 5.5 MB. World Wide Waste has no images or tables. It has almost 20% more words though. It has an epub file size of 0.35 MB. Its file size is thus nearly 94% smaller than that for Top Tasks, even though it has 9,000 more words. That's a huge weight difference. That's much lighter on the environment, less stressful, less polluting.

A reason why World Wide Waste has a much smaller carbon footprint than Top Tasks is because I was thinking about digital weight throughout the entire processes of writing and publishing. For example, I chose Times New Roman as the book font because it is a standard font. Had I chosen a custom font, that would have added extra weight. At every step in the process, I watched my weight, and it paid off.

We must always think about the weight of digital. Things can get very heavy very quickly without us noticing. Weight equals pollution. It is often unnecessary weight. It does not add any value. In digital, we are constantly negatively impacting the environment for no benefit to anyone. There's not much point in saving the planet offline if you're killing it online. Think of the weight of everything you do in digital.

I have set out to make this book the least weight possible. It is black and white, and I have not used images or charts. I have used Times New Roman as a font, which is a standard font, thus it will have less weight.

The whole process of writing and researching this book has been a major wake-up call for me. It's only a few years ago that, as I was reading about a small group of concerned citizens protesting against the opening of an Apple data center in Ireland, I was thinking to myself: "What are these fools doing? Why are they against jobs and progress? What could be wrong with a data center?"

There's a lot wrong with data centers, despite the fact that they have become much more energy efficient. The millions of computer servers that they use all require significant energy to manufacture, contributing to the mountains of e-waste and pollution. These data centers facilitate Instagram Culture which accelerates fast fashion; they facilitate Ride-Hailing Culture which accelerates congestion and pollution; they facilitate Ecommerce Culture which has accelerated the return of goods so that now it is three times higher than the rate in physical stores.

Key actions

Before you do anything in digital, think about its impact on the environment. Think about the Earth Experience, not just the user or customer experience. Focus on reducing the weight of your digital footprint. Reduce the digital waste. Before you make a decision relating to digital, ask yourself these questions:

1. What's the total lifetime impact on the environment?
2. How do we minimize this impact?
3. How do we reduce as much waste as possible?
4. Do you need to do this digitally? Do you? Do you really need to do this at all?

Links

Global warming, Wikipedia
https://en.wikipedia.org/wiki/Global_warming

Earth Overshoot Day
https://www.overshootday.org/

Living Planet Report 2018, World Wildlife Fund
https://www.worldwildlife.org/pages/living-planet-report-2018

The planet is being consumed by humans, Mark Lynas, CNN, 2019
https://edition.cnn.com/2019/08/08/opinions/planet-consumed-by-humans-intl/index.html

This is what would happen to the natural world if all the insects disappeared, Stuart Reynolds, The Conversation, 2019
https://www.weforum.org/agenda/2019/02/what-happens-to-the-natural-world-if-all-the-insects-disappear

Nature's Dangerous Decline 'Unprecedented'; Species Extinction Rates 'Accelerating', United Nations, 2019
https://www.un.org/sustainabledevelopment/blog/2019/05/nature-decline-unprecedented-report/

Global Greenhouse Gas Emissions Data, US EPA
https://www.epa.gov/ghgemissions/global-greenhouse-gas-emissions-data

Facebook Ireland staff coin it as average pay reaches €154,000, Mark Paul, Irish Times, 2018
https://www.irishtimes.com/business/technology/Facebook-ireland-staff-coin-it-as-average-pay-reaches-154-000-1.3714642

And the statistic of the decade award goes to… 0.3%, Harriet Grant, The Guardian, 2019
https://www.theguardian.com/business/2019/dec/23/statistic-of-decade-award-03-per-cent

How many species on Earth? Why that's a simple question but hard to answer, Tanya Latty, Timothy Lee, The Conversation, 2019
https://theconversation.com/how-many-species-on-Earth-why-thats-a-simple-question-but-hard-to-answer-114909

The Environmental Impact of Amazon's Kindle, Cleantech, Emma Ritch, 2009
https://gato-docs.its.txstate.edu/jcr:4646e321-9a29-41e5-880d-4c5ffe69e03e/thoughts_ereaders.pdf

Print or Digital: It All Has Environmental Impact, Omega Institute for Holistic Studies 2014
https://www.eomega.org/article/print-or-digital-it-all-has-environmental-impact

Screening environmental life cycle assessment of printed, web based and tablet e-paper newspaper, Å Moberg, M Johansson, G Finnveden, A Jonsson, 2009
https://www.csc.kth.se/sustain/publications/reportfiles/sus_2007_1_moberg_et_al_report_updated.pdf

How Green Is My iPad? Daniel Goleman, Gregory Norris, New York Times, 2010
https://archive.nytimes.com/www.nytimes.com/interactive/2010/04/04/opinion/04opchart.html

E-Books vs. Print Books: What's the Difference? Linda McMaken, Investopedia, 2019
https://www.investopedia.com/financial-edge/0812/e-books-vs.-print-books.aspx

The 2010s were supposed to bring the e-book revolution. It never quite came, Constance Grady, Vox, 2019
https://www.vox.com/culture/2019/12/23/20991659/e-book-amazon-kindle-ereader-department-of-justice-publishing-lawsuit-apple-ipad

Are reading e-books on e-Readers environmentally friendly? Michael Kozlowski, goodEreader, 2017
https://goodereader.com/blog/electronic-readers/are-reading-e-books-on-e-readers-environmentally-friendly

How Many Books Does the Average Person Read? Thomas Whittington, Iris Reading, 2016
https://www.irisreading.com/how-many-books-does-the-average-person-read/

How Many Trees Does It Take to Make a Textbook? Reference.com
https://www.reference.com/science/many-trees-make-textbook-6d5fa1f120445a74

Here's How Many Trees Humans Cut Down Each Year, Justin Worland, TIME, 2015
https://time.com/4019277/trees-humans-deforestation/

Fact Check: Are There Really More Trees Today Than 100 Years Ago? Tentree, 2017
https://www.tentree.com/blogs/posts/fact-check-are-there-really-more-trees-today-than-100-years-ago

How much CO2 do trees absorb? GoTreeQuotes
https://www.gotreequotes.com/how-much-co2-do-trees-absorb/

Trees Improve Our Air Quality, Urban forestry network
http://urbanforestrynetwork.org/benefits/air%20quality.htm

How Planting Trees Can Help Reduce Your Carbon Footprint,
onetreeplanted.org, 2014
https://onetreeplanted.org/blogs/stories/planting-trees-reduce-carbon-
footprint

How Many Trees Are There in the World? Scientific American, 2015
https://www.scientificamerican.com/article/how-many-trees-are-there-in-
the-world-video/

How Many Trees Are In The World? The Answer Will Surprise You,
Logan Strain, Green Future, 2017
https://greenfuture.io/nature/how-many-trees-are-in-the-world

Tree planting 'has mind-blowing potential' to tackle climate crisis, Damian
Carrington, The Guardian, 2019
https://www.theguardian.com/environment/2019/jul/04/planting-billions-
trees-best-tackle-climate-crisis-scientists-canopy-emissions

Scientists Zero in on Trees as a Surprisingly Large Source of Methane, Fred
Pearce, Yale Environment 360, 2019
https://e360.yale.edu/features/scientists-probe-the-surprising-role-of-trees-
in-methane-emissions

This tech company is aiming to plant 500 billion trees by 2060 – using
drones, Kate Whiting, The Conversation, 2019
https://www.weforum.org/agenda/2019/12/technology-artificial-
intelligence-ai-drone-trees-deforestation/

Junkies and wasters

Feeding the addiction

I'm an addict. I've been a junkie for about 25 years. I can't resist my morning fix. Before I do anything useful, I have to have it. And throughout the day, multiple times. My addiction is to news and all sorts of information, to the desire not to be missing out on anything, to be always on, to the desire not to be bored, to be up-to-date, to be connected, and to be reassured that I still matter because someone else somewhere has in some small way interacted with something I've said or done, and therefore confirmed that I exist, and that in some tiny, tiny way, I matter a little bit.

I have the sense that if I'm not online I'm not fully alive. I check my email multiple times a day. I'm always on Twitter. I have an in-depth knowledge of a wide range of current news stories. News, I consume news voraciously. And the idea of sticking with one publication seems simply insane. I use Google News because it's an all-you-can-read with such incredible variety. And even though I'm a news junkie, I don't want to pay for it. Funny, I love news so much I don't want to pay for it. How can I love that which I don't want to pay for? What sort of love is that?

Funny, being an addict and knowing I'm an addict and promising to change, and sometimes changing a bit for a week, or maybe sometimes for a month, but always reverting back to the same old habits. I don't want to count how much of my day I waste reading and checking stuff that I don't really need to read and check. I know I don't need to read the same news story from multiple sources with ever so slight variations. I don't need to follow the intricate details of so many events and happenings, so many of which depress me and make me feel that the world is a terrible place. It's not making me smarter or more enlightened. It's certainly not making me happier.

Why do I do it? Because I'm human. I've inherited deep and persistent human instincts and traits. More. Free. Fast. Convenient. News. Production. Ego. How can I resist what is free? How can I resist what is fast and convenient? How can I resist what has been specifically designed to be addictive? Speed is an addiction. How can I resist getting more? How can I resist producing and publishing when it's so easy and free to produce and publish? How can I resist knowing that others are talking about me, retweeting me?

This book is a journey for me. A tool to help me create a less wasteful life, and to help me reduce the negative impacts of my actions on the environment. I hope it can help you too.

Life is irony. Most of the professional work I've done for the last 25 years or so has been about helping organizations do less but do it better. I have developed a research method called Top Tasks to help understand what truly matters. I've tried to help hundreds of organizations get control of their data addictions, while not fully realizing that I have many of my own. Organizations do love to create stuff, to publish stuff, to launch stuff, to collect and store stuff.

I have worked with organizations in around 40 countries and they all have the same basic behaviors. In all my years, nobody has ever said to me: "Help us become more organization-centric. We're too focused on our customers." Organizations love themselves and there is no deeper expression of that love than in the creation and consumption of physical and digital stuff and things. And they love to collect information on their customers, even when they will never use the vast majority of that information. In fact, 90% of the data organizations create and collect they never use. It's useless data.

These ideas and issues have been rolling around in my head for years. At the same time, Rosilda, my wonderful wife, has been educating me on how to better care for our environment and to live more consciously and mindfully. Greta Thunberg and all those young climate champions were another wake-up call. I've started flying less, though still too much. I began to think about how I could play a more useful role.

Then it struck me—out of the blue—it struck me: Every time I download an email I contribute to global warming. Every time I tweet, do a search, check a webpage, I create pollution. Digital is physical. Those data centers are not in the Cloud. They're on land in massive physical buildings packed full of computers hungry for energy. It seems invisible. It seems cheap and free. It's not. Digital costs the Earth.

We don't have an energy production crisis. We do have an energy consumption crisis. We consume far too much of everything the Earth produces and in the last 40 years our appetites for everything have exploded, driven and enabled by advances in digital technology. Recycling and renewables are often a form of green-washing for big corporations. To go 100% renewable would not be without its costs, as the machines that make wind and solar technology need to be manufactured, consuming energy, the batteries in our electric cars need precious raw materials. We consume too much energy, that's the problem, and like our waistlines, these habits have gone out of control.

Whether it is correlation or causation, we can map the explosive growth of digital over the last 40 years with the explosive growth in resource depletion. Undoubtedly, massive wealth has been created for a tiny elite, with 26 people owning as much as the poorest 50% of the planet's population, according to Oxfam. While poverty reduction showed promising signs in the early years of this century, as the Web matures, progress has stalled. "An estimated 820 million people did not have enough to eat in 2018," according to the UN, "up from 811 million in the previous year, which is the third year of increase in a row."

In a paradox of sorts, the UN points out that there is also an obesity epidemic, particularly among schoolchildren. According to the OECD, there are strong signs that the middle class, particularly in Western countries, is being hollowed out. "The middle-income group has grown smaller with each successive generation," the OECD explains. "70% of the baby boomers were part of the middle class in their twenties, compared with 60% of the millennials." In the US, millions of workers are stressed and in despair, with life expectancy about four years lower than in comparable countries, according to the US Centers for Disease Control and Prevention.

Culture of waste

We might argue that digital is not responsible for the wealth or poverty. What we cannot argue with is that digital is massively, unbelievably, wantonly wasteful. Forget about everything else, digital is killing our planet with waste. The World Wide Web is indeed the World Wide Waste. The dark side of digital is that it has been a massive accelerant for our desire to create and own stuff, to consume, dispose of, and waste time, resources and energy at never-before-dreamt-of levels.

We are ravaging the planet to satiate exploding wants, desires, whims. We are laying waste to our Earth at a speed that has become mind-boggling. And digital itself is wanton waste upon waste. Many smartphones and other digital products are deliberately designed with custom screws and bonded glues to make them difficult or impossible to repair, to be the ultimate in single-use thinking, and to be incredibly difficult to recycle. All for profit. The short-term growth club. Amazon knows that the less time we have to wait, the more we'll buy, and the more we'll buy of things we don't really need. Digital is turning us into screaming babies: we want it and we want it now!

Up to 90% of digital data is not used. We collect. We store. We create and then don't use. Data is the atomic structure of digital. Words, music, images, films, videos, software. It all ends up as data. Most data is like single-use, throwaway plastic. What sort of society accepts 90% waste?

- Around 90% of data is never accessed three months after it is first stored, according to Tech Target.
- 80% of all digital data is never accessed or used again after it is stored, according to a 2018 report by Active Archive Alliance.
- Businesses typically only analyze around 10% of the data they collect, according to search technology specialist Lucidworks.

- 90% of unstructured data is never analyzed, according to IDC.
- 90% of all sensor data collected from Internet of Things devices is never used, according to IBM.

We download the free app, try it maybe once, and then never again. Research by mobile intelligence firm, Quettra, found that the average app loses 77% of its users within the first three days after the install, 90% within the first 30 days, and 95% within the first 90. All that effort, expense and energy that went into creating things that nobody is using. The energy it cost to download for that one single use. But it's okay because it was free. Free costs the Earth. Few business models are causing more long-term damage to our environment than the "free" model because it is based on the twin evils of waste and advertising.

Look inside most organizations and you will see that they are monstrosities of digital waste. "My experience is that IT landscapes are 90% waste," Wolfgang Goebl, founder of the Architectural Thinking Association, told me. "What I've seen in many companies is that they could run the same business with 10% of IT applications and servers."

While humans love to produce and collect data, we hate to organize, to sift, to edit, to clean up the data waste. Making stuff useful is not something we seem to be good at or want to do. Digital has sold us the dream that all that hard, difficult, grindy work, we don't need to do it anymore. We can store everything and the search engine or the artificial intelligence (AI) will sort it out. That's a big, huge lie. It's one thing to be using raw materials from this planet in the pursuit of producing things that might actually have some use. But to destroy this beautiful planet in the pursuit of producing digital crap? Shame on us.

We must overcome the pervasive idea that digital removes from us the responsibility to organize things and to clean up after ourselves. This is a truly deep, pernicious and corrupting idea.

I once had a chat with a manager who was about to retire. He reminisced about how as a young manager—before personal computers— he would get sent on courses about how to organize his office, his filing cabinet. Once he got a computer, these courses stopped when they should have been ramped up, because as he admitted himself, he now had hundreds of filing cabinets' worth of information to sort through. But the organization he worked with had bought into the false idea that computers not simply stored and processed information, but had some sort of magical organizing function too.

I have found it almost impossible to get any organization I worked with to properly invest in professionally managing search and findability on their intranets. They will buy the search engine, they will buy the content management system, but they will not pay for the professional management of the information. They refuse. They have this magical thinking that you buy the software and then find the lowest-paid worker in the department to add the content.

Even on public websites it has been a massive struggle. Only the most progressive managers were interested in investing in information architecture, navigation and findability. And it is a total rarity to find an organization that has a truly professional approach to reviewing and removing out-of-date content.

Our waste production has not just got faster. It has got **explosively** faster. 90% of data that has been created in the entire history of human civilization was created between 2017 and 2019. Can you imagine that? In two years we created more data than in all previous history, 90% of which is crap. From the Iliad to the Bible to Magna Carta, all the stuff we've created throughout history, in two short years we have created more than all humans created before 2017. Think about that for a moment.

We are the crap-producing society. Crap production is what our age will be remembered for the most. It's accelerating. According to the World Economic Forum, annual waste generation is predicted to increase globally by 70% between 2016 and 2050. A study by the University of Natural Resources and Life Sciences, Vienna, found that we have dumped 2,500 gigatons (a gigaton is 1,000,000,000 metric tons) of waste and pollution into the environment since 1900, with 28% of this happening between 2002 and 2015. So, in a little more than 10 years of the new century, we produced almost a third of the waste we produced in the previous 90 years.

Under certain circumstances, e-commerce could be better for the environment than driving to the store. But if e-commerce encourages unnecessary consumption, then it will be worse. Research compiled by Shopify in 2019 from eMarketer, Star Business Journal, and Forrester, estimated that while brick-and-mortar returns are in the range of 8–10%, e-commerce returns average out at 20%. David Sobie, co-founder of Happy Returns, a network of physical return locations, estimated that apparel returns can be as high as 30%, and that at holiday times online returns can reach 40%.

Transporting returned products in the US creates over 15 million metric tons of CO_2 pollution every year, according to Optoro, a logistics optimization firm. We'd need to plant 1.5 billion trees to deal with that amount of pollution. Not just that, about 2.5 million tons of these returned goods are then dumped, creating even more pollution.

E-commerce packaging accounts for 30% of solid waste generated in the US, according to the US Environmental Protection Agency. About 165 billion packages are shipped in the US each year. That's a billion trees' worth of cardboard, according to data from USPS, FedEx, and UPS analyzed by LimeLoop. If 20% of e-commerce purchases are returned, then there are 200 million trees being cut down every year to deal with the passing whims of US consumers alone.

I remember once chatting with someone running a 300-page website. She was stressed because it was a lot of pages to manage properly, and she was getting constant requests to publish new pages. A couple of years later, I met her again and she was in quite good form. I asked her how many pages there were now on the website. "Thousands," she replied. "In fact, I've lost count." I was surprised and I asked her if she didn't feel even more stress now. "Not really," she said. "I just accepted it. I publish whatever people ask me to publish now. Before it was more stressful because I was constantly arguing with people about what should and shouldn't be published. Now I publish, and nobody expects me to review a website this big."

That's it. I've seen this behavior so many times, and, of course, I've seen this behavior many times in myself. When it gets to a certain level of bigness, you give in and go with the flow—or the flood. When you overload, you pass the threshold of caring. We have surrendered to digital excess.

When you've got thousands of pages, what's one more page? It's a problem you feel you can't deal with, so you ignore it, and hope it goes away, and after a while you stop even thinking about it. Then you wonder why you can't find stuff, or why stuff is out of date, or why you've spent the last five minutes reading something that should never have been published in the first place. We can and must do something about it.

Zettabyte Armageddon

From 1997 to 2017, global Internet traffic in data increased by a factor of 1.7 million, according to Cisco. That sort of increase is hard to even fathom. It's not that unusual though to see huge increases in data production once the tools allow it. Data expands to meet the space available.

The printing press massively accelerated data production. "In the year 1550 alone, for example, some 3 million books were produced in Western Europe, more than the total number of manuscripts produced during the fourteenth century as a whole," Eltjo Buringh and Jan Luiten van Zanden wrote in their paper Charting the "Rise of the West."

In 2018, 33 zettabytes of data were created. By 2025, it's estimated that there will be 175 zettabytes, and that by 2035 there will be more than 2,000 zettabytes, according to Statista.

Okay, so I know you're dying to ask how big a zettabyte is. You know a gigabyte is a lot, right? Yeah, it used to be megabytes. Megabytes were big. But then the gigabytes stomped all over them because the gigabyte is 1,000 megabytes. But a zettabyte is a trillion gigabytes. Yes, a trillion, which is a thousand billion. Let's try and put a zettabyte into the context of books and trees.

Let's start by estimating how many pages in an average book. Richard Lea, writing for The Guardian in 2015, reported on a number of studies that indicated that fiction books had increased in length from around 300 pages in 1999 to around 400 pages in 2015. On the other hand, it seems non-fiction books are getting shorter. "As recently as 2011, the average book length of the #1 non-fiction bestseller was 467 pages. By 2017, however, that number has dropped to 273 pages," Tucker Max wrote for Scribe in 2017. Taking the fiction and non-fiction figures and averaging them gives us an overall average of 350 pages for a typical book.

An average tree provides approximately 8,333 sheets of copy-type paper, based on analysis by Conservatree. Thus, one tree can provide about 47 copies of a 350-page book. Decoline Shipping estimated that one tree would yield about 62 books. TAPPI, a paper industry trade group, estimated a typical tree will yield about 30 books.

Let's say an average tree produces 50 350-page books and that on each of those pages there are between 250 and 300 words. That gives us about 100,000 words per book or five million words per tree. I tested how many KB was used for saving 100,000 words in a couple of formats and got an average of 500 KB. Let's throw some images and tables into the mix and bring the size up to 1 MB, which would mean that an average tree stores the equivalent of 50 MB of data.

A zettabyte is 1,000,000,000,000,000 MB or one quadrillion MB. If a zettabyte was printed out in 100,000-word books, with a few images thrown in, then we would have one quadrillion books. It would take 20,000,000,000,000 (20 trillion) trees' worth of paper to print these books. It is estimated that there are currently three trillion trees on the planet. To print a zettabyte of data would thus require almost seven times the number of trees that currently exist to be cut down and turned into paper.

We could give every one of the 7.7 billion people on this planet 129,870 of these books. They'd have almost 13 billion words to read. An average reader can read 1,000 words in about five minutes. It would therefore take 752 years of non-stop, no-sleep reading for every man, woman and child on the planet to read a zettabyte. One zettabyte. There were 33 zettabytes of data created in 2018 alone, and by 2035 it is estimated that there will be over 2,000 zettabytes.

In 2010, Google Books estimated that there were about 130 million unique book titles published. Mental Floss estimated that there are roughly 800,000 books published every year globally. My own rough calculations from Wikipedia data came to about 900,000 per year. Let's be generous and say that there are about one million unique titles published each year. That would mean that by 2020 there were about 140 million unique titles published throughout history.

"The average book in America sells about 500 copies," Chris Anderson wrote for Publisher's Weekly in 2006. Steven Piersanti, President of Berrett-Koehler Publishers, stated in 2016 that total sales for a typical non-fiction book are no more than 2,000 copies. An average of the two figures gives us 1,250 copies. If we multiply that by 140 million, we get 175 billion copies of books published since publishing began.

Summarizing all these crazy calculations we can say that one zettabyte—one zettabyte—if printed out would create 6,000 times more print than all the books that have ever been printed. The sheer scale of the amount of digital data that is being created and stored is quite simply mind-boggling. 90% of each zettabyte is useless crap. Why?

Because we can. Because it's easy. Because it's cheap. At least, it seems cheap. A megabyte is a lot of data. A gigabyte is a whole lot of data. Based on calculations I will go into in detail later, the transfer of one gigabyte (GB) of data requires about 0.015 kWh of electricity and causes 0.0042 kg of CO_2 pollution. In the grand scheme of things, that's a very inconsequential figure. As the gigabytes pile up it begins to register on the pollution monitor, though. When we get into zettabytes, there are real and substantial pollution consequences.

How much pollution does the transfer of 2,000 zettabytes of data cause?

8,400,000,000,000 kg. Eight trillion, four hundred billion kilos.

How many trees would you need to plant to absorb that amount of pollution?

840,000,000,000. Eight hundred forty billion.

Now we're talking real numbers, aren't we?

A tree is a lousy hard disk. It can only "store" about 50 MB of data. We can buy a USB stick for $10 that stores 64 GB. That's 1,300 times more storage on a thing that fits on our key ring and is so light we won't notice any extra weight. The brain begins to think that digital is limitless, that digital is as light as air, that digital is as cheap as nothing. That's not true. Digital has a weight, and because there's so much digital data—so enormously much—it is weighing heavier and heavier on our planet.

I'm just talking about the data here. The devices required to create, transmit and store this data require multiples of energy to manufacture. The production of these devices is also exploding. They live very short lives and then they are mainly dumped, creating mountains of toxic waste.

The zettabytes of data that we create are 90% useless crap. They are like massive container ships of crap moving back and forth across the Internet, spewing out huge amounts of filthy pollution.

We must invest massively more in the skills of organizing and analyzing data. Even more critical skills we need to develop are the not-producing-crap-in-the-first-place skills. Or the skill of not saving so much crap. Or the skill of deleting the stuff that wasn't crap but is now crap. And then there's the skill of knowing which data we put into cold storage or into the archive or whatever we want to call it. Most of the data we need to store, say for legal reasons, will rarely if ever be accessed, so we can put it into deep low-energy storage, which can save up to 90% in energy costs.

Cheap. In digital we have lost the concept of value. One of the core underlying problems of society is that our current economic model makes it so easy and cheap to produce, publish and store digital (and physical) stuff.

In 1956, the IBM 350 storage disk drive was the size of a large wardrobe and stored about 3.75 MB of data. You could rent it for $3,200 per month. In 1967, a one-megabyte hard drive cost about one million US dollars. That meant that content writers really thought about the words and images needed. It meant that software developers really thought about every line of code they wrote. By 2020, Google Drive was offering 15 GB of storage for free and 100 GB for $1.99 per month.

From something that cost a million to something that costs nothing; that is a truly mega drop. Digital, it's like sugar. Sugar used to be a scarce resource, then it became abundant and we gorged on it.

Cheap storage combined with cheap processing power made the World Wide Web the World Wide Waste. The Web is an ocean full of crap. We live on the first page of search results, never venturing forth beyond the first few results, so we don't see all the crap lurking underneath. More people have been on top of Mount Everest than have been to the 10th page of search results. Parents warn their children: "Don't go beyond the first page of search results." I searched for "climate change." Google informed me that there were "about 931,000,000" results. That's 931 million results! Who visits all these pages? A 2018 study by Ahrefs found that 91% of all pages they analyzed got zero traffic from Google. What's the point? What-is-the-point?

It's cheap to store so we store up the problem. When we save ourselves time in the present, the future pays. On the shallow surface, the cost of storing something digital is much less than the cost of editing it, cleaning it up, and getting rid of it after it is no longer useful. We keep making these false calculations of how much time we can save right this very moment if we store the stuff instead of spending time editing it, but we're storing up problems for the future. We must start calculating the true cost of digital, and that means calculating the total costs of digital products and data over their entire lifetime. Storage is one element of data's cost. When you're looking through 10,000 photos for that one that really matters, those 9,999 other photos are costing you your time and energy and ability to focus.

Knowledge transfer, not data transfer

In the traditional technology industry, data and information have traditionally been seen as storage or transmission challenges. The question is "How do we store this data?" rather than "Should we store this data?" or "How do we use it?" There's a deep history here. In the roots of computer science is the concept that data and information are things, units, bits and bytes. In this worldview, 1,000 bytes is 1,000 bytes—one byte is the same as another. Humans love to store.

Cheap feeds the addiction of wanting more than we need. If the history of humans were told as a 24-hour clock, for the first 23 hours and 50 minutes, we would have lived a hungry, famine-riven, spartan existence. For the last ten minutes, cheap food would have flowed and many of us would have gone from malnourished to obese, from spartan dwellers to obsessive hoarders.

Throughout modern history, famine has been a brutal teacher that has taught us to crave more. More food. More land. More energy. More of everything and anything we could lay our hands on. Digital makes us super-hoarders. A megabyte is like an acre of land. Every year, the amount of digital land we can use gets cheaper and cheaper, so we buy more land and store more stuff there. It's so hard to resist more.

There is another way of thinking about information and data. It goes back to the ancient Greeks and Romans. It sees information not so much as a noun (a thing) but rather as a verb. It sees data and information as a process of helping shape and form the mind, as the act of communicating intelligence or knowledge. In this world, information exists once it is known and understood within the mind of the person who has received it.

The value for a piece of information, from an ancient Greek point of view, would not be measured from the perspective of the creator or the communicator, but rather from the perspective of the receiver. In this worldview, information only becomes information when it is understood, when it has delivered some form of intelligence, knowledge or value.

If someone asked you the time and you tell them the wrong time, that's not information. If you start talking about the weather instead of telling them the time, that's not information. If they asked you the time in English and you tell them the time in Japanese, that's not information. Their knowing the right time after talking to you is information.

We must change from a culture of want to a culture of use. Want creates waste. Use creates usefulness. We must measure value based on how well the data is used and understood. Then, we will have much less data and much better data, since we'd have to spend much more time managing the data because we'd be measured based on how useful the data is, not based on how much data we've produced. When it comes to data, we must stop measuring outputs and start measuring outcomes. Has the knowledge been transferred? Can the person act on it?

A circular economy

We live in a linear economy. The aim is to make the thing and sell the thing or publish the thing and then pretty much forget the thing. In our linear economy, waste is not the responsibility of the producer. This irresponsibility is having catastrophic impacts on our environment. In our linear economy, recycling is at best a bandage, at worst it's a PR stunt.

The linear economy has been enabled by cheap and seemingly abundant raw materials. Once manufacturers have no responsibility to continuously manage these materials throughout their entire life cycle, once they can create waste and have no responsibility for that waste, then things like single-use plastic and hard-to-repair-and-recycle smartphones become the logical outputs.

We have an energy consumption crisis, not an energy production crisis. We need to radically slow down our energy use and our waste production. Innovation in digital, whether it is Artificial Intelligence, Virtual Reality, driverless cars or high-definition TVs, tends to have exponentially rising demands in energy. In a world in crisis, digital is a runaway train.

We need a circular economy. "A circular economy is based on the principles of designing out waste and pollution, keeping products and materials in use, and regenerating natural systems," the Ellen MacArthur Foundation explains. We need circular economy thinking.

Once there was a big plant that was polluting a river. They gave the problem to a group of children. The plant needed clean water as part of its manufacturing process. The children decided that the plant's waste water should enter the river before the point where the plant took in its clean water. The waste water had to turned into the clean water that the plant needed to manufacture its products. The plant was forced to turn its waste water into clean water.

Here's some circular thinking:
1. You make it, you own it forever. It's never old. You must take it back. Your old products become the raw material from which you build your new products.

2. You create data, you own it forever. You must look after it until the moment it is deleted. Any data without an owner gets automatically deleted.

3. You are measured on outcomes not inputs. What positive outcomes were you responsible for today?

Key actions

Cut the crap. Reduce the produce. Decrease the consume. Before you create or collect data, before you acquire a digital device, ask yourself these questions:

- Do I really, truly need this?
- Is there something I already have that I can use instead?
- Am I willing and able to dispose properly of this after it is no longer useful?

Links

Demand for cold data storage heats up, Marc Staimer, Tech Target, 2017
https://searchstorage.techtarget.com/feature/No-data-left-behind-Demand-for-cold-data-storage-heats-up

Dark data and why you should worry about it, Ian Barker, betanews, 2018
https://betanews.com/2016/02/19/big-dark-data/

What Your Data Isn't Telling You: Dark Data Presents Problems And Opportunities For Big Businesses, Mary Meehan, Forbes, 2019
https://www.forbes.com/sites/marymeehan/2019/06/04/what-your-data-isnt-telling-you-dark-data-presents-problems-and-opportunities-for-big-businesses/

Dark data, Wikipedia
https://en.wikipedia.org/wiki/Dark_data

Unstructured data, Webopedia
https://www.webopedia.com/TERM/U/unstructured_data.html

IDC Study Uncovers Best Practices in Unlocking the Hidden Value of Information, IDC, 2014
https://www.businesswire.com/news/home/20140715005986/en/New-IDC-Study-Uncovers-Practices-Unlocking-Hidden

Unstructured Data and the 80 Percent Rule, Seth Grimes, Breakthrough Analysis, 2013
http://breakthroughanalysis.com/2008/08/01/unstructured-data-and-the-80-percent-rule/

On average, between 60% and 73% of all data within an enterprise goes unused for analytics. Mike Gualtieri, Forrester, 2016
https://go.forrester.com/blogs/hadoop-is-datas-darling-for-a-reason/

How Much Data is Created on the Internet Each Day? Jeff Schultz, Micro Focus, 2019
https://blog.microfocus.com/how-much-data-is-created-on-the-internet-each-day/

How Big is Big Data? Przemek Chojecki, Medium, 2019
https://towardsdatascience.com/how-big-is-big-data-3fb14d5351ba

The concept of information, Rafael Capurro, Birger Hjørland, 2003
http://www.capurro.de/infoconcept.html

Cisco Visual Networking Index: Forecast and Trends, 2017–2022, Cisco, 2019
https://www.cisco.com/c/en/us/solutions/collateral/service-provider/visual-networking-index-vni/white-paper-c11-741490.html

91% of Content Gets No Traffic From Google, Tim Soulo, Ahrefs, 2018
https://ahrefs.com/blog/search-traffic-study/

77 percent of users never use an app again 72 hours after installing, John Dye, Android Authority, 2016
https://www.androidauthority.com/77-percent-users-dont-use-an-app-after-three-days-678107/

Nearly 1 in 4 people abandon mobile apps after only one use, Sarah Perez, TechCrunch, 2016
https://techcrunch.com/2016/05/31/nearly-1-in-4-people-abandon-mobile-apps-after-only-one-use/

The Plague of Ecommerce Return Rates and How to Maintain Profitability, Aaron Orendorff, Shopify, 2019
https://www.shopify.com/enterprise/ecommerce-returns

The Growing Problem of Customer Returns, Marcia Kaplan, Practical Ecommerce, 2019
https://www.practicalecommerce.com/the-growing-problem-of-customer-returns

Free returns come with an environmental cost, Marcia Kaplan, Practical Ecommerce, 2019
https://www.theverge.com/2019/12/26/21031855/free-returns-environmental-cost-holiday-online-shopping-amazon

Can Online Retail Solve Its Packaging Problem? Adele Peters, Fast Company, 2018
https://www.fastcompany.com/40560641/can-online-retail-solve-its-packaging-problem

World's 26 richest people own as much as poorest 50%, says Oxfam, Larry Elliott, The Guardian, 2019
https://www.theguardian.com/business/2019/jan/21/world-26-richest-people-own-as-much-as-poorest-50-per-cent-oxfam-report

World hunger is still not going down after three years and obesity is still growing – UN report, WHO, 2019
https://www.who.int/news-room/detail/15-07-2019-world-hunger-is-still-not-going-down-after-three-years-and-obesity-is-still-growing-un-report

Under Pressure: The Squeezed Middle Class, OECD, 2019
https://www.oecd.org/els/soc/OECD-middle-class-2019-main-findings.pdf

US life expectancy has been declining. Here's why, Uptin Saiidi, CNBC, 2019
https://www.cnbc.com/2019/07/09/us-life-expectancy-has-been-declining-heres-why.html

US life expectancy climbs for the first time in 4 years as drug overdose and cancer deaths decline, Jacqueline Howard, CNN, 2020
https://edition.cnn.com/2020/01/30/health/us-life-expectancy-drug-overdose-deaths-cdc-study/index.html

Global Resources Outlook: 2019: Natural Resources for the Future We Want, United Nations, 2019
https://internationalresourcepanel.org/reports/global-resources-outlook

Focusing on cutting emissions alone won't halt ecological decline, we must consume less – former UK chief environmental adviser, Ian Boyd, The Conversation, 2019
https://theconversation.com/focusing-on-cutting-emissions-alone-wont-halt-ecological-decline-we-must-consume-less-former-uk-chief-environmental-adviser-122778#Echobox=1567440386

From resource extraction to outflows of wastes and emissions: 1900–2015, F. Krausmann, C. Lauk, W. Haas, D. Wiedenhofer, Science Direct, 2018
https://www.sciencedirect.com/science/article/pii/S0959378017313031

For a true circular economy, we must redefine waste, Alexandre Lemille, The Conversation, 2019
https://www.weforum.org/agenda/2019/11/build-circular-economy-stop-recycling

Where's the productivity?

Productivity matters

I remember the swooshing, grating sound as the sharpening stone slid down the blade of the scythe, removing any dirt, grime or rust. Back and forth, one side then the other, my father's hand wielded the stone until the blade shone. It was time to cut the hay and we were poor farmers. We couldn't afford the farm machinery. But soon even we were forced to give up on the scythe and hire a neighbor to cut our few fields of hay. That's because cutting a field of hay with a scythe took forever.

It's estimated that before the introduction of farm machinery "an able-bodied laborer could reap about one quarter acre of wheat in a day using a sickle," according to Wikipedia. With farm machinery, "two men and two horses could cut, rake and bind 20 acres of wheat per day." 10.10.20, I still remember the name of the fertilizer that brought nitrogen, phosphorus, and potassium to our soil. In the years before we used 10.10.20 we'd get about five cocks of hay from a field. After applying it, we were getting more than 20.

It was easy to see productivity gains when a farm started using machinery and fertilizers. They were dramatic, and they were the difference between having a life of subsistence and being able to afford a few small luxuries, a better education, and a way out of the grind of existence.

The typewriter was something. I had advanced from scrawly writing. I would stay up many a late night two-fingering its keys, trying to master the art of Tipp-ex, cursing when I had not waited long enough for it to dry and the hammered key splodged the page. How I longed for a word processor. Finally, I got enough money together and waited for the January sales. For the last three or four days of December, I walked quite the distance to peer in through the shop window at the machine of my desires. To bring it home. To open the box, set it up and start typing. What a thrill! And then to graduate to a computer and to have Microsoft Word. And so on and so on. The pen was my scythe. The computer was my machinery. Or was it?

Too many emails

Experts have been claiming that email "died" during the early 2000s because of the advent of all sorts of new communications channels such as texting, Facebook, Slack, etc. For something that is dead, it sure as hell shows lots of signs of life. According to Statista, there will be over 300 billion emails sent and received every single day in 2020. That's over 30 billion more a day than were sent in 2017.

Let's say a knowledge worker can send two letters a day when using pen and paper. With a computer they can send 40. Does that make them more productive? Using fertilizer and cutting the field using machinery literally changed my life. Sending 40 emails versus two emails should make us more productive. But what if 20 of those emails are unnecessary? That's a waste of time, isn't it? Yes, and not just for the writer, but also for the people who receive them and have got to respond. Email. Even though I can't live without it, it can be a problem.

A 2019 study found that in the UK there are 64 million unnecessary emails sent every day. It estimated that if everyone sent one less "thank you" email, there would be 16 UK tonnes less carbon emitted in a year. One less email every day in the UK alone would mean saving 2,750 trees from having to deal with unnecessary pollution.

According to Mike Berners-Lee's 2010 book How Bad are Bananas?, the average email creates 4 grams of CO_2. (Yes, he's the brother of Tim, inventor of the Web.) An email with an attachment creates as much as 50 grams of CO_2. Simply receiving a spam causes 0.3 grams (0.0003 kg) of CO_2.

About half of all emails are spam, according to Statista. That would mean that every year about 55 trillion spam emails are sent, creating about 16 billion kg of CO_2. You would have to plant about 1.6 billion trees to offset its pollution. 1.6 billion. Something is surely wrong with a system that allows criminals to destroy the planet while conning the world for free.

Unfortunately, spam has nothing on legitimate emails when it comes to pollution. You would have to plant 21 billion trees to deal with the pollution caused by sending typical emails, and this is not accounting for the percentage of emails with attachments. A Harvard study of CEOs found that almost a quarter of their time was spent dealing with emails. Some years ago, we did a Top Tasks analysis of management in one of the world's largest companies. When we asked them what was the most time-consuming part of their jobs, email was way out in front. When we asked them what activity added the most value, email was way down the list.

Back in 2012, those tech visionaries at McKinsey saw the problem and knew the solution to email. It's always the same solution: more technology. New technology. New communications software had the potential to increase employee productivity by a whopping 25%! "The average interaction worker spends an estimated 28% of the workweek managing email and nearly 20% looking for internal information or tracking down colleagues who can help with specific tasks," McKinsey wrote.

Good job Slack and Teams and G Suite were just down the yellow brick techie road promising innovation and life-changing, productivity-enhancing sign-on-the-bottom-line enhancements. Fast forward to 2019. "On average, employees at large companies are each sending more than 200 Slack messages per week," Rani Molla wrote for Recode in 2019. He was referencing data from Time Is Ltd., a productivity analytics company. Power users sending out more than 1,000 messages per day were not an exception, according to the analysis.

We're still children when it comes to digital. We want new toys all the time. "We're just moving email to another place and it's less searchable," Sarah Peck, founder of Startup Pregnant, stated about Slack et al. Slack is instant. Slack is always on. Great. Email is stressful. Slack is super-stressful.

Digital never gets tired. Digital is relentless. Digital is much more a producer than an organizer. The tool shapes us so we must become always on, always producing. We slowly morph into the most-used features of our software.

We're not software. We don't work well in always-on mode. We get tired. We get distracted. We need periods of quiet so as to truly concentrate and be productive. Think before you send that message. Consider that you are interrupting the flow of your colleagues. Slow down. Turn off. Wait. Before creating an email or a Slack message, think about the environments: the work environment and the planetary environment. Don't add to the pollution. Instead of trying to go fast, fast. Get in control. Your brain is still quite useful. Use it more. Stop outsourcing your thinking to Google, Slack, email, etc.

Technology productivity paradox

For most of civilization humans lived pretty miserable lives. Any sort of productivity improvement was eaten up by a growing population. About 150 years ago, certain countries began to progress rapidly. Immediately after the Second World War, productivity really took off. "Today the average person on the planet is as rich as the average person in the richest country in 1950," Max Roser wrote for Our World In Data in 2020. By any measure, that is extraordinary progress. However, as digital rose in prominence, that progress began to slow and then stall.

During the 1970s and 1980s, when computing power had increased 100-fold in the United States, productivity growth dropped from an average of 3% per year in the Sixties to 1%. From the mid-Nineties, it picked up again, getting close to levels seen in the Sixties. However, after the great recession of 2007–08, it fell off a cliff again. "Real median disposable income in the United States was lower in 2012 than it was in 2000," Jason Furman, Chairman of US Council of Economic Advisers, stated in 2015.

In 2019, The Conference Board, a global business research organization, released a report stating that in the 123 countries it monitored, productivity had remained weak in 2018 and would continue to be slow in 2019. "The long-awaited productivity effects from digital transformation are still too small to see reflected in a lasting improvement at the macroeconomic level," said Bart van Ark, Global Chief Economist of The Conference Board. It's not just productivity that has declined. "The average US firm's return on assets has progressively dropped 75% since 1965," the World Economic Forum reported in 2020.

Why has digital innovation not resulted in a surge in productivity? Why, with the exception of the mid-Nineties, did the opposite occur? According to The Shift Project, for every $3–5 spent on digital, we get $2 back in productivity. In the UK, they've had their worst decade for productivity since the early 1800s, with an anemic 0.3% productivity growth. The 0.3% figure "is probably the most important UK statistic of the last decade," Hetan Shah, executive director of the Royal Statistical Society, stated.

Crap destroys productivity

Reusing waste can increase productivity. Useless waste is unproductive. If you're looking for an underlying reason why digital has not delivered on its productivity promise, it's because digital has delivered too much useless waste. If we want to improve productivity, we have to cut the crap.

90% of digital is waste, whether it's wasted content, wasted design, wasted code, or e-waste piling up in some toxic dump. The adage "garbage in, garbage out" is still the truest of true sayings. We create too much crap data and we create too much crap software. Mixing crap data and crap software gets you more crap. You can personalize it, you can AI it, you'll still get crap. You can't polish a turd.

If an organization has an ineffective culture for the creation and management of data, then all technology will do is accelerate bad habits. To someone who deals in crap, giving them content management software is like taking away their shovel and giving them an e-shovel. They're going to shovel crap faster.

If an organization has an ineffective culture of communication, adding a new communications technology to the mix adds a new crap-making machine. If an organization has a culture of being internally competitive (as very many traditional organizations are), giving them collaboration software isn't going to do much.

You can't have digital transformation if you don't have organizational transformation. Let's face it, the vast majority of organizations are appallingly bad at organizing data, information, and content in a way that is usable and useful. They are also not great at organizing effective teams and true collaborative environments.

In my work on intranets, the biggest improvements we saw were not down to buying new technology. They were a result of changing organizational behavior. We made people responsible for the content they published. We greatly reduced the number of publishers, gave them better training, and got them collaborating with each other. We incentivized sharing, got people to write content using words that their colleagues would use when searching. We trained people about the critical importance of metadata and how to write it better.

"Periods of outsized productivity growth do not necessarily align with periods normally associated with technological innovation," Jason Furman wrote. How we as humans organize ourselves has tremendous productivity potential. Even if the technology is genuinely new and innovative, we must also have a new organizational structure and way of working and thinking to get the best out of it.

You cannot create a collaborative culture if employees are rewarded only for individual effort. You cannot get departments working together if they are all competing for budgets and prestige with each other. You cannot get employees to want their content to get found on the intranet if it is their belief that getting found means getting more work, getting more questions from employees outside their department, knowing that answering these questions will often be frowned on by their manager because it's not furthering the department's objectives.

The biggest productivity improvement of all I have been associated with was when we convinced the organization to cut the crap. When we did a massive cull of 80% of the crap data that was on the intranet, a whole world of productivity blossomed.

We don't need more digital innovation. No, please stop, you're killing me with your latest app. Enough. What we desperately need is organizational innovation, new ways of working, new ways of collaborating, new ways of thinking about society and economy. The old model was hierarchical. The new model is collaborative, team-based and cross-functional.

Digital's big lie

I have watched digital technology being sold into hundreds of organizations over 25 years. There is one constant, recurrent lie that both the buyer and seller tell each other. It is that digital is self-organizing. You pay the hefty price tag, plug it in and then watch all those efficiencies blossom. Oh, forgot, you have to fire lots of people as well. The business case for so much technology and software is that you can get rid of lots and lots of people.

Among the people who are to be fired are those who help organize and manage the flow of information throughout an organization. They may be secretaries, editors, office managers, librarians, information architects. Fire them all and then the knowledge workers who are left can book their own meeting rooms, claim their own expenses, do their own research, moderate their own conversations and group collaborations.

It is magical thinking based on three tremendously false assumptions:

1. That software organizes data on its own. Even the vaunted artificial intelligence (AI) can't do that because if the base data that AI learns from is crap, then everything after it is crap.

2. That the software will be so easy to use that it will require hardly any training or effort. Designing easy-to-use software is still a rare skill. Nine out of ten software environments that I have come across exhibited shockingly bad usability.

3. That all knowledge workers are natural communicators and collaborators. That they don't require ongoing guidance and support in order to develop quality data and collaborative skills. Nurturing communication and collaboration skills have never been more essential.

Key actions

Cut that crap. Delete at least 80%. Right now, crap, useless data is destroying organizational efficiency. We must cut the crap, and that begins by adopting new ways of collaborative working.

Links

Productivity paradox, Wikipedia
https://en.wikipedia.org/wiki/Productivity_paradox

The productivity pit: how Slack is ruining work, Rani Molla, recode, 2019
https://www.vox.com/recode/2019/5/1/18511575/productivity-slack-google-microsoft-Facebook

Global Productivity Growth Remains Weak, Extending Slowing Trend, The Conference Board, 2019
https://www.prnewswire.com/news-releases/global-productivity-growth-remains-weak-extending-slowing-trend-300831848.html

How Bad Are Bananas?: The carbon footprint of everything, Mike Berners-Lee, Profile Books, 2010
https://www.goodreads.com/book/show/7230015-how-bad-are-bananas

Pointless emails: they're not just irritating – they have a massive carbon footprint, Stephen Moss, The Guardian, 2019
https://www.theguardian.com/technology/shortcuts/2019/nov/26/pointless-emails-theyre-not-just-irritating-they-have-a-massive-carbon-footprint

The Carbon Cost of an Email, Emma Charlotte, Carbon Literacy Project, 2018
https://carbonliteracy.com/the-carbon-cost-of-an-email/

An analysis of CEOs' schedules scrutinized 60,000 hours and found email is an even bigger time sink than people realize, Myelle Lansat, Business Insider, 2018
https://www.businessinsider.com/email-dangerous-time-sink-for-ceos-study-2018-6

The social economy: Unlocking value and productivity through social technologies, McKinsey, 2012
https://www.mckinsey.com/industries/technology-media-and-telecommunications/our-insights/the-social-economy

Global Growth: Modest Pickup to 2.5% in 2020 amid Mounting Debt and Slowing Productivity Growth, World Bank, 2020
https://www.worldbank.org/en/news/press-release/2020/01/08/modest-pickup-in-2020-amid-mounting-debt-and-slowing-productivity-growth

Productivity Growth in the Advanced Economies, Jason Furman, US Council of Economic Advisers, 2015
https://obamawhitehouse.archives.gov/sites/default/files/docs/20150709_productivity_advanced_economies_piie.pdf

Economic Growth, Max Roser, OurWorldInData.org, 2020
https://ourworldindata.org/economic-growth

And the statistic of the decade award goes to… 0.3%, Harriet Grant, The Guardian, 2019
https://www.theguardian.com/business/2019/dec/23/statistic-of-decade-award-03-per-cent

The Global Productivity Slowdown: Diagnosis, Causes and Remedies, G. Erber, U. Fritsche, P. Harms, Intereconomics, 2017
http://www.iea-world.org/wp-content/uploads/2017/07/Intereconomics.pdf

Humane leadership must be the Fourth Industrial Revolution's real innovation, Paolo Gallo, Vlatka Hlupic, The Conversation, 2019
https://www.weforum.org/agenda/2019/05/humane-leadership-is-the-4irs-big-management-innovation

CEO compensation has grown 940% since 1978. Typical worker compensation has risen only 12% during that time, Lawrence Mishel, Julia Wolfe, Economic Policy Institute, 2019
https://www.epi.org/publication/ceo-compensation-2018/

Not healthy

Management failure

I think of so many digital projects I've worked on where after months and sometimes years of work, effort and progress, some newly appointed manager decided to change, to start from scratch again simply for the sake of changing, of showing that they were doing something. I have often seen a manager decide not to use a particular design or piece of research, even though their team might have spent months of effort on it, or not to fix a blatant flaw in usability that was coming up month after month, year after year.

Waste. Countless digital initiatives stopped on a whim or a bout of ego. I know the phrase about not throwing good money after bad, but this wasn't that sort of thinking. It was someone somewhere deciding that they didn't need this thing anymore, or that on second thought this initiative was going to be too hard to push through, or that they didn't feel like moving forward with the project. Or their boss walked into the room and said the project needed more "innovation," "interactivity" or "wow" factor.

In other words, it needed that special something app of bullshit that would make this boss look good when they presented it for 30 seconds in front of the board. Some bullshit video or bullshit carousel or some bullshit content droning on about how the organization was so excited and cared so much about making things simpler. (What can be less exciting than hearing that an organization is "excited"?)

In large organizations the crap-makers, the waste-producers, often rise to the top. It's not simply the poor management. Many involved in digital—and I am very much thinking about myself here—rarely gave a second thought to the fact that a huge amount of energy was expended creating these designs and this content and this code, and we shouldn't just throw it away or leave it there to rot.

And it rots. The bad code rots the good code because it makes the good code harder to understand, and it makes it harder for the good code to work because it gets in the way and slows things down and corrodes. It's a vital skill to get rid of things because they don't work, to prune things, to remove the old code or content that once was fresh and now is stale. But that's not what happens.

We leave so much stuff in Zombieland—not quite dead but not alive either. In reality, nothing really gets thrown away. The designs that with a bit of extra refinement would work great are stored somewhere because we might need them again sometime, except we never will. We must change. We must decide what must be deleted, removed, thrown away, and delete it. We must make the effort to understand what can be reused and reuse it.

These are vital skills that are currently lacking among digital professionals and management in general.

When technology systems don't work, they don't get ripped out and properly replaced. Instead, they get left there when the new one is bought until there's multiple half-baked training systems, and multiple half-baked document management systems, and multiple this and multiple that, until it's a giant big rotting mess of inefficiency, where most of the time and money has to be spent on maintaining the hulking monster that nobody fully understands because the people who wrote critical elements of the code left 10 years ago and didn't leave proper notes on how the code worked, or if they did they left notes that are so cryptic and bewildering that dipping into the bowels of the monster feels like the mission of a bomb disposal expert.

And here's the thing: management doesn't care. They never did. We wouldn't have 90% crap if we didn't have 90% crap management. Traditional management has failed. Digital is too much for it, beyond its realms of understanding. Traditional management has been bred to subcontract and outsource. "That's an IT issue. Let's give them the budget and they can deal with it." For too long that was the management mantra: not my responsibility.

In the teeming galaxy of massive, outrageous enterprise software mega-disasters, the Canadian government Phoenix payroll system is one small star. Like every single one of these disasters, it was supposed to save millions and millions when it was launched in 2015. There were great photo ops with ribbons being cut. Staff responsible were given awards.

It immediately crashed and burned. Tens of thousands were left without being paid properly. It was a typical unmitigated enterprise software disaster, totally predictable. Anyone with quarter of a brain would have seen it coming light years away. Instead of saving the Canadian government millions, it is estimated Phoenix will cost Canadian taxpayers over $2 billion to fix. Yes, that is TWO BILLION. Waste.

Why? The relentless focus was on buying and launching the thing, instead of creating an environment, supported by software, that made it easier to manage pay. We must stop focusing on having more things and on ribbon-cutting opportunities. We must focus on the outcome. We must focus on the use.

On another level, these managers are technology groupies. They totally bought into the magical thinking that if they buy the "right" technology, it will solve everything, and that the biggest problem in the modern organization is—wait for it—people. People are the problem that technology "solves." That's why productivity sucks. You still need people who have the skills to make decisions about what data to keep and what data to get rid of, who have the skills to create and nurture an efficient collaborative environment, who can head off conflict before it develops, who can gently keep everyone on message and focused.

We have bred a breed of managers who have little interest in making it easier for employees to do their jobs because at heart they're people-firers. How can they care about people, how can they care about making things useful for employees, when business school has trained them to be the job killers and cost cutters? In the frigid minds of these "managers," every new technology or innovation is judged through the cost-cutting, people-firing lens. To them, agile software design isn't about making better, simpler software. Agile is instead another way to cut corners and save costs.

In more than twenty years of working in multiple industries, and working for hundreds of organizations, I struggle to remember a single senior manager who genuinely cared about making things easier to find and easier to do on their intranet. The result? It's so much harder for employees to find what they need to do their jobs, to understand what they need to do their jobs, to get the best quality information available to do their jobs. Thus, time leeches away, productivity leeches away.

Management has been trained to focus on the new and the short-term, rather than the existing and the long-term. Go to the vast majority of websites and what do you see? A barrage of messages, offers, and deals for "potential" customers. Some of these deals are exclusively for "potential" customers; current customers need not apply. If they're lucky, current customers will have a tiny login in the top-right corner of the page. Current customers are treated almost as badly as employees.

Why is this? Because it's hard to stand out by caring for and supporting current customers. After all, these aren't even "your" customers. Someone else got them. Managers are bred and trained on much harder stuff than that. It's a war out there, according to management culture. You need to have a military marketing and advertising "campaign" where you "target," "capture" and "win" more new customers. Once having "won" these customers, they're yours. Why would you care about them? They're the spoils of war, the bounty you receive after a successful campaign. They're your prisoners, and that's essentially how current customers are treated in a great many organizations.

Too many managers

You would expect that with declining productivity and declining return on assets, management as a discipline would be under pressure. Quite the opposite. As organizational performance has rapidly declined, senior management pay has skyrocketed. "CEO compensation has grown 940% since 1978," according to the Economic Policy Institute, while "typical worker compensation has risen only 12% during that time." Failure and poor performance have never had much of an effect on senior management pay, it seems. When Boeing fired CEO Dennis Muilenburg in 2019 for the 737-Max fiasco, he walked away with over $60 million.

The story of the US healthcare system over the last 50 years tells us a lot about why digital and managers have failed to deliver on their many promises contained in their many emails and PowerPoints. Between 1975 and 2010, the number of practicing physicians in the US grew 150%, while the number of health administrators and managers grew by 3,200%, according to an Athena Health analysis.

Not surprisingly, healthcare costs increased from "0.8 percent of the economy in 1970 to 3.1 percent by 2000 and 5.4 percent in 2017," according to the US Committee for a Responsible Federal Budget. "Federal health spending has grown by 230 percent since 2000, while economy-wide prices have only risen 40 percent, and the economy has only grown by 90 percent." With all this new technology and all this new management, the US healthcare system has become hugely inefficient.

"With less than 5% of the world's population, the US now accounts for 40% of global health spending, almost twice as much per capita as the next highest-spending country," Shannon, Joseph Colucci, and Thom Walsh wrote in 2013. Since 1980, the gap between life expectancy in the US and that in comparable countries has increased, according to analysis by the Kaiser Family Foundation.

Why?

US healthcare focuses on technology, on activities, and work for managers. It focuses on organizational inputs, not patient outcomes. According to Brownlee et al., the tests and treatments become ends in themselves. Patients are recommended to undergo particular treatments simply because "resources such as beds and technology are available."

This is profoundly stupid. This goes to the essence, the core of why digital has accelerated waste production. Digital is being used to create inputs in the form of treatments and tests. Digital is then being used to vomit up endless useless data on the useless treatment that the useless administrators use to create useless PowerPoints so that they can present in useless meetings, and then listen to other useless data from other useless administrators. Inputs, inputs, inputs. Keep them busy.

If we measured patient outcomes, we would radically reduce waste and deliver much better products and services. Did they get better? How long did it take them to get better?

Why don't we measure patient outcomes?

Jobs for managers. The inputs demand a lot of useless management. The inputs create a lot of metrics and digital is absolutely fantastic at creating reams and reams of useless metrics data. The more you manage the inputs, the more you paralyze the system because you begin to manage the minutiae of nothingness. Your focus goes further and further away from what really matters.

Is the patient getting better? Did the treatment work?

Enter Buurtzorg

If you are a social care nurse who goes out into the community to help people, chances are a huge digitally based administrative system has grown up around you that is measuring everything you do. It can measure how many minutes you spend with each patient, how long it takes you to change a bandage, to wash someone, to take their temperature. I saw a documentary once that showed a nurse as she bent down to tie the shoelaces of an old person in her care. "Now, I am delivering Product 67," she said to the cameras. Everything the nurse did was measured.

Of course, the fact that there are lots of measurements means that there is lots of management. There will be dashboards and reports and lots of meetings; lots of management stuff. You'll hear about how there's been a 7% reduction in the bandage-changing time in the last quarter, and how shoelaces are now tied in an average of 30 seconds instead of 33. Lots of "management." Lots of waste.

In 2008, a Dutch home-care organization called Buurtzorg was formed. They had four staff and a radical idea. Get rid of managers and instead empower the nurses. Stop all the silly measurement of inputs. Instead, measure what mattered. Buurtzorg asked the essential question: What is the most important thing to a patient? The answer: To live a healthy, independent life. Healthy, independent living became the key metric.

All the other micro-metrics that measured the nurse were thrown away. The nurses were trusted again. When a nurse met a patient for the first time, they were encouraged to get to know them and to build up their social network by talking to friends, neighbors and family. That would never have happened in the old system, where talking to the children and neighbors would not have been possible because it couldn't be directly mapped to an activity input such as changing a bandage. A nurse was only allowed X amount of time per visit. Talking to a neighbor would have been seen as a waste of time.

Buurtzorg threw out the old model and focused on the outcome of independent living. Now, if a nurse noticed that someone's laces were untied, they didn't just mechanically bend down and tie them. They'd keep an eye on things and if it began to become a regular occurrence, they'd talk to the patient, trying to figure out why. Did the person need more exercise? Perhaps the nurse might try and organize for them to go swimming or do yoga or maybe do some physiotherapy.

Buurtzorg charges more per hour for their nurses than competitors. Yet they have the lowest overall cost for care in the Netherlands, and their patients spend the least time in hospital. They have the highest patient satisfaction and the highest employee satisfaction. They have grown from four nurses in 2008 to 14,000 in 2019. And they have done it all by having hardly any managers. There are fewer than 100 at headquarters. It's all about small, independent, empowered teams of 10–14 people who are constantly sharing best practice.

Why does it work? Why is it better than the old system of having huge numbers of managers and administrators and measuring inputs? Because if you are allowed the freedom to think, if you are allowed to address why someone can't tie their shoelaces, they are less likely to trip and have an accident. If you spend the time to build the social network around the person, then that network can be an ongoing support. If they need to go swimming, then you might know a neighbor who could bring them.

This is a model that shows us that we can create a better environment for almost everybody; less wasteful, more productive, with more satisfaction for all. Just as digital fed the old environment of input, it can facilitate the new customer-outcome-focused environment too. Teams are at the heart of the Buurtzorg model and isolated teams quickly become ineffective ones. The teams try to meet face-to-face on a daily basis, but they also use technology to keep in touch, share best practice, learn, collaborate, evolve.

Digital gives the tools of organization to small teams that were historically the domain of larger, hierarchical structures. In a complex environment, the team is increasingly showing that it is wiser, more adaptive, more productive than the individual and the traditional manager model. We must use digital to liberate the collective intelligence rather than to reinforce the old hierarchical structures.

The world has changed. Organizations have not. The number one rule at Buurtzorg is that the nurse must spend the majority of their time with their patients. In the many organizations I have dealt with, digital has become a wall between the organization and its customers, patients, citizens. Traditional organizations have used digital to focus on the internal mechanics of the organization. Fewer and fewer employees have any contact with the people they are supposed to serve. How can that be good?

Digital has in many ways eliminated geography. That doesn't mean it has eliminated distance. Sometimes, employees are emailing or using Slack when they could get up off their chairs, walk over and have a face-to-face chat. Knowing your customers involves more than knowing their data.

Digital must empower teams to get closer to their customers. Digital design should occur "with" the customer, not be done in some back room "for" them. The further away the producer gets from the consumer, the more waste will occur. The closer the producer to the consumer, the less waste and the better the work.

As UX researcher, Cyd Harrell, has stated, "People are better at their jobs when they can see the effect their work has on other people." When you have such great distance between producer and consumer, then it is so easy to create meaningless features and to focus your attention on meaningless work inputs.

The customer keeps you honest and can help you design in a way that is frugal and purposeful, keeping you constantly focused on the outcome, and thus constantly focused on true value.

Key actions

Measure the outcome for the person using the product or service. What use is it to them? What is their experience? However, don't forget the Earth Experience. What is the outcome for the Earth?

Links

Rally marks four years of Phoenix Pay System problems, Katie Griffin, CTV News, 2020
https://ottawa.ctvnews.ca/rally-marks-four-years-of-phoenix-pay-system-problems-1.4830737

CEO compensation has grown 940% since 1978. Typical worker compensation has risen only 12% during that time
https://www.epi.org/publication/ceo-compensation-2018/

Productivity and the Health Care Workforce, S. Brownlee, J. Colucci, T. Walsh, 2013
https://www.researchgate.net/publication/276267924_Productivity_and_the_Health_Care_Workforce

American Health Care: Health Spending and the Federal Budget, US Committee for a Responsible Federal Budget, 2018
https://www.crfb.org/papers/american-health-care-health-spending-and-federal-budget

How does U.S. life expectancy compare to other countries? S. Gonzales, M. Ramirez, B. Sawyer, Peterson-KFF, 2019
https://www.healthsystemtracker.org/chart-collection/u-s-life-expectancy-compare-countries/?_sf_s=life#item-start

Life expectancy in the US keeps going down, and a new study says America's worsening inequality could be to blame, Aylin Woodward, Business Insider, 2019
https://www.businessinsider.com/us-life-expectancy-declined-for-third-year-in-a-row-2019-11?r=US&IR=T

US life expectancy is still on the decline. Here's why, Jen Christensen, CNN, 2019
https://edition.cnn.com/2019/11/26/health/us-life-expectancy-decline-study/index.html

German nursing shortage in hospitals – Homemade by Profititis? Björn Brücher, Daniela Deufert, European Academy of Sciences and Arts, 2019
https://www.euro-acad.eu/library?id=6

The Buurtzorg Model, Buurtzorg
https://www.buurtzorg.com/about-us/buurtzorgmodel/

How to make your online shopping more environmentally friendly, Stuart Milligan, Baris Yalabik, The Conversation, 2019
https://theconversation.com/how-to-make-your-online-shopping-more-environmentally-friendly-123117

Energy drain

Manufacturing energy

Estimating the total energy that digital consumes is not easy because digital is everywhere and in practically everything. For example, a new car or truck "can have up to 100 networked microprocessors running 150 million lines of code with thousands of supporting active components," Jeff Darrow writes for Electronic Design. As the digital Web gets further embedded with Internet of Things (IoT), digital will become woven into everything from our clothes to our food.

The energy demand of digital is "growing by 4% per year, in stark contrast to the trend of global GDP's energy intensity evolution, which is declining by 1.8% per year," a Shift Project report stated in 2019. "The explosion of video uses (Skype, streaming, etc.) and the increased consumption of frequently renewed digital equipment are the main drivers of this inflation." In a world of climate change, where much of the world is trying to reduce energy use, digital's hunger for energy is growing.

There are three major areas where digital consumes energy:

1. Manufacture
2. Use
3. Waste

It used to be that the things we made (cars, fridges) used more energy during their lifetime of use than during the period of their manufacture. For example, a car can last from eight to 15 years, according to US Consumer Reports, whereas the lifespan of a computer is typically three to five years, and the lifespan of a smartphone is typically two to three years. In general, the more use you get out of something, the better it is for the environment. "If you make a car last to 200,000 miles rather than 100,000, then the emissions for each mile the car does in its lifetime may drop by as much as 50%, as a result of getting more distance out of the initial manufacturing emissions," Mike Berners-Lee and Duncan Clark wrote for The Guardian in 2010.

To manufacture something made of steel or plastic requires "between 1 and 10 megajoule[s] of electricity per kilogram of material," explains Kris De Decker, editor of Low-Tech magazine. However, to manufacture a semiconductor requires between 1,000 and 100,000 megajoules per kilogram of material. In 2011, researchers from Arizona State University found that of the total energy consumed by a computer during its lifetime, 70% of that is consumed during its manufacture. In 2019, Ethical Consumer reported that the manufacturing stage for a typical smartphone can create up to 80% of its total pollution.

It is thus nearly always better to keep using a digital device than to change it for a newer version. A huge amount of pollution was released making the phone in your hand and the computer on your table. Try to get the maximum possible use out of it. It's greener to use than to buy new. And when you buy, buy for quality, buy things that will last. Cheap costs the Earth. There's nothing worse for the planet than throwaway digital devices.

Energy during use

Over time, digital products have generally become a lot more energy efficient. A typical data center in 2019 was a lot more efficient than its equivalent in 2010. A study published in Science in 2020 found that while the computing output of data centers globally grew sixfold from 2010 to 2018, their energy consumption only rose by 6%. However, because of the explosion of data and digital devices, the OECD reported that in OECD countries pollution caused by digital had grown by about 450 million tons since 2013, while "overall OECD CO2 pollution actually decreased by 250 million tons."

According to a report from New York University's AI Institute, the technology sector (excluding TVs and consumer electronics) would cause 3.6% of global greenhouse gas pollution in 2020, more than double what it caused in 2007. In a worst-case scenario, this figure could rise to 14% by 2040. In 2019, the Financial Times reported that digital "contributes to about 4 per cent of global greenhouse gas pollution... 37% higher than what it was in 2010."

Digital pollution was the equivalent to that of the fuel used by the aviation industry in 2018, according to an article by Nicola Jones in Nature. She was reporting on research by Anders Andrae which estimated that by 2030, in a best-case scenario, digital would be consuming 8% of global electricity, and in a worst case, it could be 21%. What could accelerate the worst case? "If the computationally intensive cryptocurrency Bitcoin continues to grow," Jones wrote, "a sharp rise in energy demand could come sooner rather than later." (More on Bitcoin later.)

An even bigger problem will be if the rest of the world tries to catch up with US pollution habits. In 2018, US energy consumption per person was about four times what an average citizen of the world would consume, according to the US Energy Information Administration. Driven by IoT, the number of connected devices is exploding, and connectivity equals electricity. According to Cisco:

- In the United States, there will be an average of 13.6 networked devices per person by 2022, up from 8.1 in 2017.

- In China, there will be 4.4 networked devices per person by 2022, up from 2.8 in 2017.
- In India, there will be 1.5 networked devices per person by 2022, up from 1.2 in 2017.
- Globally, there will be 3.6 networked devices per person by 2022, up from 2.4 in 2017.

We have an ever-growing hunger for data, particularly "rich" data, such as videos, and we want higher and higher resolutions. Netflix estimates that when you're streaming in standard definition, you're using about one GB per hour. However, if you're using high definition, that jumps to up to three GB per hour. If you double the definition you usually treble the weight, and much of this definition is wholly unnecessary because you can't see the difference. It's useless waste.

According to Cisco:

- In the United States, Internet traffic will grow 3.1-fold from 2017 to 2022, an annual growth rate of 25%. Average traffic per person per month will grow from 120.2 GB in 2017 to 304.6 GB in 2022.
- Globally, average traffic per person per month will grow from 16.2 GB in 2017 to 49.8 GB in 2022.
- In China, average traffic per person per month will grow from 15.6 GB in 2017 to 66.1 GB in 2022.
- In India, average traffic per person per month will grow from 2.4 GB in 2017 to 13.9 GB in 2022.

Let's say someone is using 140 GB of data a month. What sort of pollution is that causing? That's not an easy question to answer. If you search about data energy usage, then you're likely to find studies that state that transmitting and storing one gigabyte of data consumes 7 kWh, or 3.9 kWh or 0.06 kWh: a huge variance. You will find that the 7 kWh figure is quoted quite a bit, but if you dig deeper you will find that the study this figure is based on was published in 2009, and that networks have become much more energy efficient since then.

Here lies a data integrity problem. Not much gets archived or deleted on the Web. Wrong and out-of-date information is everywhere. Older content often comes up earlier in search results than fresher, more recently published content. As Norbert Wiener stated in 1950, "The idea that information can be stored in a changing world without an overwhelming depreciation in its value is false." As the Web gets older, more and more of it becomes "fake" because the information it seeks to communicate is no longer accurate. You have to do your homework if you want to get close to the facts.

Turns out that the 0.06 kWh is a figure published in 2015 that was based on a review of multiple other studies and seems to be the more accurate one. According to this analysis, the amount of energy required to transmit and store data has been decreasing by half every two years since 2000. Extrapolating that trend outwards to 2019, we get a figure of 0.015 kWh per GB, and that is the figure I will use for this book.

Thus, a monthly data usage of 140 GB per US citizen comes to 2.1 kWh or about 0.59 kg of pollution. The population of the US is 327 million. So, every year US citizens' data production and consumption habits emit about 2.4 billion kg of CO_2. You'd need to plant 230 million trees to deal with that pollution. By 2022, Cisco estimates it will be 304 GB per person per month. We'd need to plant over 500 million trees to deal with that.

Digital continues to develop technologies that have massive energy needs. Blockchain is a technology that uses the network to allow secure, transparent and anonymous transactions to occur. It is an alternative to the traditional banking system, as value, transactions and communications are authenticated, not by one central authority, but by all the members of the network. It is a truly interesting idea with tremendous potential, but its energy needs are huge.

Bitcoin is an example of a cryptocurrency using blockchain. Bitcoin is a "decentralized digital currency without a central bank or single administrator that can be sent from user to user on the peer-to-peer bitcoin network without the need for intermediaries," according to Wikipedia. Creating bitcoins, which is called "mining," creates huge amounts of pollution. Nature magazine has estimated that the mining of Bitcoin and similar cryptocurrencies consumes more energy than most other minerals of an equivalent market value. Basically, mining a dollar's worth of Bitcoin is more expensive than mining a dollar's worth of gold. As well, a cryptocurrency transaction costs as much in energy as hundreds of thousands of Visa-type transactions. Blockchain and cryptocurrencies need to become much more energy conscious and environmentally friendly.

Many tech companies are aware of the environmental issues and are seeking to make digital devices and data centers more energy efficient. A lot of the more advanced data centers use substantial quantities of renewable energy, and their energy efficiency improved dramatically between 2010 and 2020. This is good but it's not addressing the core issue, which is overconsumption. We consume too much digital, way, way too much, and it's exploding, exploding, exploding. The business case of so many in digital is overconsumption. The more we consume of digital, the more money they make. Let's say we eat too much ice cream. Well, the tech industry is telling us: "Hey, look, we've found more energy-efficient ways to make ice cream!"

This idea that because it's renewable we can use as much as we want is a dangerous one, and unfortunately feeds the myth of digital, which is all about unlimited power, space and energy. In the psychology of the Internet, cyberspace has no boundaries, has no weight, and the information superhighway goes on and on without end, without limit. There is an end, though, and there is a weight.

Every single thing that happens in digital has an energy cost that is charged to the Earth. Every byte of data takes the Earth's energy to create and takes the Earth's energy to transit and store. The windmills and solar panels that make our renewable energy all need to be manufactured, transported, installed, maintained and retired. That all creates pollution. The renewable energy they create needs to be transmitted across creaking electrical infrastructure and will feed billions of hungry digital machines that were themselves manufactured and will ultimately become waste; some of the worst and most toxic waste ever to have been created.

"It's the most powerful greenhouse gas known to humanity, and emissions have risen rapidly in recent years," the BBC reported in 2019. "Sulphur hexafluoride, or SF6, is widely used in the electrical industry to prevent short circuits and accidents. But leaks of the little-known gas in the UK and the rest of the EU in 2017 were the equivalent of putting an extra 1.3 million cars on the road." Wind turbines use SF6.

E-waste

"Electronic waste or e-waste describes discarded electrical or electronic devices," according to Wikipedia. As of 2019, 50 million tons of e-waste were being produced each year, with smartphones accounting for as much waste as desktops, laptops and displays combined. All the commercial aircraft ever built come to about 50 million tons of material. If one year's e-waste was laid out together, it would cover an area the size of Manhattan. That's one year's waste. It's estimated that by 2050 we will be producing 120 million tons of e-waste a year.

E-waste is more destructive to the environment than many other forms of waste because:

1. Short lifespans (typically less than five years) mean that tech churns through raw materials at a tremendous pace.
2. High manufacturing energy costs mean that the tech products cause most of their pollution during the manufacturing process. Combine that with their short lifespans and you get a perfect storm of pollution.
3. The culture of tech is the culture of change, newness, innovation. The business model depends on super-short lifespans for hardware

and software. For the tech industry, growth comes through waste. In tech, nothing is built to last. Everything is built to waste because the driving idea is that there is a new innovation around the corner that will change everything.

4. Many digital products are deliberately designed not to be repaired. Smartphones are often designed with special glues, custom screws and batteries that can't be easily replaced.

5. Much e-waste includes toxic materials that are harmful to the environment.

6. E-waste tends to involve a highly complex mix of materials, thus making it difficult and costly to recycle.

In 2020, the European Parliament voted overwhelmingly in favour of introducing a single universal charging method for mobile phones. The Parliament estimated that obsolete cables generate more than 51,000 tonnes of e-waste per year. What was Apple's response? "Regulations that would drive conformity across the type of connector built into all smartphones freeze innovation rather than encourage it," an official statement from the company read. "Such proposals are bad for the environment and unnecessarily disruptive for customers." In 2020, we surely live in a world of Orwellian doublespeak. In some tech circles, innovation has become a god, a god that sacrifices the Earth in pursuit of newness and change.

In 2016, according to the US Environmental Protection Agency, only about 12% of e-waste was recycled in the US. The UN estimated that in 2016 about 20% of e-waste was recycled globally. These figures are low but then recycling has always been a bit of a PR mirage, a way industry can market itself as being environmentally conscious. Recycling does not address the core problem: overproduction and overconsumption. Recycling can be like going to mass on a Sunday, thinking it gives a license to be an asshole for the rest of the week.

Digital facilitates a culture of waste because it is a key driver in the world of convenience. Digital is always saying to us: "Don't spend your physical energy. Spend my electrical energy." Any digital appliance that uses a standby mode constantly wastes energy. Instant-on televisions, computers in sleep mode, cable set-top boxes that are never turned off, and game consoles, all silently suck energy.

In the US, it's estimated that this "vampire power" can account for up to 20% of a typical electricity bill. According to a 2015 study by the NRDC, energy use by inactive devices costs "$19 billion a year—about $165 per US household on average—and approximately 50 large (500-megawatt) power plants' worth of electricity." The study found that the average US house has 65—yes, 65—devices permanently plugged into electrical outlets. How on Earth are you going to manage 65 devices? That's the thing. You're not. It's overload. Too many devices. Too much stuff. So much that you don't even think about it anymore.

Spending the wrong energy

"Even now, I still go to the hospital to keep receiving treatments for my arm, and there's still pain. The pain gets especially bad when it rains, but I grit my teeth and work through that." If you think that this sounds like someone with repetitive stress injury from spending too long using a computer, you'd be right. This is the voice of Lee "Flash" Young Ho, regarded as one of the legends of electronic gaming, also known as e-sports.

In 2019, there were more than 400 million fans of e-sports, and that is expected to rise to 1.1 billion by 2021. The PC and game consoles that Lee "Flash" Young Ho plays are super-hungry consumers of energy. "Globally, PC gamers use about 75 billion kWh of electricity a year, equivalent to the output of 25 electric power plants," Bryan Schatz wrote for Grist. You'd need to plant 7.2 billion trees to deal with that sort of pollution.

A study by the British Journal of Medicine of e-sports athletes found that they spent up to 10 hours a day practicing before competitions. 40% did not do any physical exercise, with 15% reporting that they sat for more than three hours without standing. Sitting "raises your risk of heart disease, diabetes, stroke, high blood pressure, and high cholesterol," according to WebMD.

E-sports embodies the modern digital world: the human body is spending less and less energy, the Earth is spending more and more. Digital is the babysitter. In interacting with digital, the human body is not working in any way like it was designed to work over millions of years. The body is largely passive, a shell for the mind, except for repetitive movements of the arms and eyes. The body's surplus energy is increasingly being stored as fat.

We are spending electrical energy instead of physical energy and are making the Earth sick and ourselves sick. A US study published in 2019 found that, by the age of eight, children were becoming much more sedentary, and that there was an even bigger drop off in exercising by age eleven. Globally, over 80% of school-going adolescents are not getting enough regular exercise, a 2019 World Health Organization study found.

Digital feeds laziness. Electric scooters that are appearing in many cities are a perfect example of devices that encourage laziness and convenience, litter sidewalks and streets, causing accidents, while damaging the environment. Researchers at North Carolina State University found that nearly half of e-scooter riders would have biked or walked had the scooters not been available. Only 34% had chosen the e-scooter instead of using their car. When everything was taken into account, the e-scooters were producing more greenhouse-gas pollution per passenger mile than a standard diesel bus with high ridership.

Digital feeds congestion and pollution. According to a 2020 report by the Union of Concerned Scientists, ride-hailing has resulted in declining mass transit ridership and increased congestion. "Ride-hailing trips today result in an estimated 69 percent more climate pollution on average than the trips they displace," the report stated. In the false economy of digital, the costs to the environment are rarely calculated. Instead, digital has become our go-to source for energy. Why go to the bother of repairing something when it's cheaper and more convenient to replace it with a more powerful version? Why get up and turn the light off when digital can do it for you? Digital feeds our addictions. Not surprisingly, you are likely to find a digital addict with one hand on the mouse and one hand clutching a sugar-saturated drink. Sugar, without doubt the greatest single addiction of the human race, tells us a harsh story of what happens when our addictions control our lives.

Key actions

Use less electrical energy. Use more of your own physical energy.

Links

The United Nations Global E-waste Monitor 2017: Quantities, Flows, and Resources, United Nations, 2017
http://ewastemonitor.info/

The world's e-waste is a huge problem. It's also a golden opportunity, Guy Ryder, Houlin Zhao Houlin, World Economic Forum, 2019
https://www.weforum.org/agenda/2019/01/how-a-circular-approach-can-turn-e-waste-into-a-golden-opportunity/

American trash: How an e-waste sting uncovered a shocking betrayal, Colin Lecher, The Verge, 2019
https://www.theverge.com/2019/12/4/20992240/e-waste-recycling-electronic-basel-convention-crime-total-reclaim-fraud

What's the carbon footprint of... a new car? Mike Berners-Lee, Duncan Clark, The Guardian, 2010
https://www.theguardian.com/environment/green-living-blog/2010/sep/23/carbon-footprint-new-car

Climate change: Electrical industry's 'dirty secret' boosts warming, Matt McGrath, BBC, 2019
https://www.bbc.com/news/science-environment-49567197

AI Now 2019 Report: Technology CO2 emissions estimate, AI Now Institute, 2019
https://ainowinstitute.org/AI_Now_2019_Report.pdf

Quantum computing could change the way the world uses energy, Vern Brownell, QUARTZ, 2019
https://qz.com/1566061/quantum-computing-will-change-the-way-the-world-uses-energy/

The Energy and Carbon Footprint of the Global ICT and E&M Sectors 2010–2015, Jens Malmodin, Dag Lundén, ResearchGate, 2018
https://www.researchgate.net/publication/327248403_The_Energy_and_Carbon_Footprint_of_the_Global_ICT_and_EM_Sectors_2010-2015

Total Consumer Power Consumption Forecast, Anders S.G. Andrae, ResearchGate, 2017
https://www.researchgate.net/publication/320225452_Total_Consumer_Power_Consumption_Forecast

Cloud Computing Is Not the Energy Hog That Had Been Feared, Steve Lohr, The New York Times
https://www.nytimes.com/2020/02/27/technology/cloud-computing-energy-usage.html

Recalibrating global data center energy-use estimates, E. Masanet, A. Shehabi, N. Leil, S. Smith, J. Koomey, Science, 2020
https://science.sciencemag.org/content/367/6481/984

Assessing ICT global emissions footprint: Trends to 2040 & recommendations, Lotfi Belkhir, Ahmed Elmeligi, Science Direct, 2018
https://www.sciencedirect.com/science/article/pii/S095965261733233X?via%3Dihub

Just because it's digital doesn't mean it's green, FT Alphaville, 2019
https://ftalphaville.ft.com/2019/03/06/1551886838000/Just-because-it-s-digital-doesn-t-mean-it-s-green/

Lean ICT: Towards digital sobriety, The Shift Project, 2019
https://theshiftproject.org/en/article/lean-ict-our-new-report/

What is the United States' share of world energy consumption? US Energy Information Administration, 2019
https://www.eia.gov/tools/faqs/faq.php?id=87&t=1

Cisco digital forecasts 2017 – 2022, Cisco
https://www.cisco.com/c/en/us/solutions/collateral/executive-perspectives/annual-internet-report/white-paper-c11-741490.html

Why We Need a Speed Limit for the Internet, Kris De Decker, Low Tech Magazine, 2015
https://solar.lowtechmagazine.com/2015/10/can-the-internet-run-on-renewable-energy.html

The monster footprint of digital technology, Kris De Decker, Low Tech Magazine, 2009
https://www.lowtechmagazine.com/2009/06/embodied-energy-of-digital-technology.html

Ride-Hailing's Climate Risks, Union of Concerned Scientists, 2020
https://www.ucsusa.org/sites/default/files/2020-02/Ride-Hailing%27s-Climate-Risks.pdf

How energy vampires could be sucking your electricity dry and costing you money, Allconnect, 2019
https://solarsam.com/solar-news/how-energy-vampires-could-be-sucking-your-electricty-dry/

Video games consume more electricity than 25 power plants can produce, Bryan Schatz, Bryan Schatz, Grist, 2018
https://grist.org/article/video-games-consume-more-electricity-than-25-power-plants-can-produce/

In this guide we investigate, score and rank the ethical and environmental record of 14 desktop computer brands, Tom Bryson, Ethical Consumer, 2019
https://www.ethicalconsumer.org/technology/shopping-guide/desktop-computers

The Micromobility Mirage, Frederic Filloux, Medium, 2019
https://mondaynote.com/the-micromobility-mirage-a814e6e126be

Computer factories eat way more energy than running the devices they build, Michael Cooney, Network World, 2011
https://www.networkworld.com/article/2229029/computer-factories-eat-way-more-energy-than-running-the-devices-they-build.html

Managing the health of the eSport athlete: an integrated health management model, J. DiFrancisco-Donoghue, J. Balentine, G. Schmidt, H. Zwibel, BMJ, 2019
https://bmjopensem.bmj.com/content/5/1/e000467

Why Sitting Too Much Is Bad for Your Health, WebMD
https://www.webmd.com/fitness-exercise/ss/slideshow-sitting-health

Children's Sport Participation and Physical Activity Study, Sports Ireland, 2019
https://www.sportireland.ie/research/news/the-first-all-island-childrens-sport-participation-and-physical-activity-study

One in three children 'not active enough', finds sport survey, BBC, 2018
https://www.bbc.com/news/health-46456104

Children around the world not getting enough exercise, report says, Tauren Dyson, UPI, 2018
https://www.upi.com/Health_News/2018/11/26/Children-around-the-world-not-getting-enough-exercise-report-says/8401543250503/

Young Children are Getting Less Exercise than We Thought, Cleveland Clinic, 2019
https://newsroom.clevelandclinic.org/2019/05/10/young-children-are-getting-less-exercise-than-we-thought/

Big sugar, big data

The oldest of cravings

Sugar is a cautionary tale of what can happen when an addictive energy source that used to be very scarce becomes cheap and abundant. Sugar is also a cautionary tale about the fragility of data, of how quickly it can go out of date, of how it can be corrupted, manipulated and misused. Sugar is the ultimate story of modern "branding," of how something sweet on the surface can have such a sour and dark underbelly.

There is nothing we crave more than energy because energy is life. Sugar is one of the most ancient and deepest of our cravings for energy. How we have responded to the explosive growth of cheap sugar has many similarities to how we have responded to the equally explosive growth of cheap digital.

Our ape ancestors adored the sugar they found in fruits and honey because sugar has two uniquely powerful properties. Firstly, it gives you an immediate energy boost. You take it and bang! you feel it acting. Like digital, sugar acts as speed. Secondly, what sugar energy you don't immediately consume is very efficiently converted into fat. In prehistoric times, there were many periods of severe hunger and famine, so our ape cousins learned to love and crave sugar because getting enough of it often meant the difference between life and death.

Over millions of years, a sugar craving was hardwired into our DNA. The pleasure centers of our brains were taught to light up at its taste. Sugar used to be as rare and precious as computing power. Our ancestors learned that whenever they got an opportunity they should gobble up as much sugar as they could get. This was the case for most of human existence.

In the thirteenth century, it would have cost about 360 eggs to buy a pound of sugar, according to Gary Taubes. In the last 200 years, we've become fabulously good at producing sugar, the price plummeted, and demand soared. In 2012, over 50% of US citizens consumed 180 pounds a year.

Sugar has a cruel and bitter history. Of the roughly 13 million slaves brought across the Atlantic, two-thirds of them worked on sugar cane plantations. There are some parallels with digital here too. Many of the raw materials that make our digital devices are mined by poor people in poor countries, by child laborers in war zones, working in toxic and dangerous conditions, so that we can have vibrant colors in our smartphone screens, so that our batteries will last longer.

Like digital, sugar is everywhere. It is hard to buy a processed product today that is not literally saturated with sugar and smothered in single-use plastic. Sugar makes everything more addictive and the profits are clear.

Wholesome foods such as vegetables tend to yield profits of 3–6%, whereas highly processed, sugary foods can yield as much as 15%. As with Facebook, the business model of sugar is addiction, stoking our deepest and most ancient cravings.

Big Sugar advertising has been used with great efficiency to trap children. There are four dominant categories for TV ads aimed at children, three out of four of which are sugar-saturated: toys, cereals, candy and fast foods. In recent years, the targeting of children—particularly poor children—has exploded. By 2020, marketing budgets in the US targeted at children were 150 times bigger than in the 1980s, while portion sizes in US restaurants have increased fourfold since the 1950s. Making poor children fat and sick is a Big Sugar advertiser's dream.

Not surprisingly, by 2016 almost 40% of the US population was obese. In 2019, the World Health Organization estimated that almost one-third of the world's population were either overweight or obese. It's not just obesity that sugar is linked to. Even at much, much lower quantities than we consume today, sugar triggers a whole range of disorders, from diabetes to cancer, according to Gary Taubes, author of The Case Against Sugar.

Dodgy data

Before there was Big Data there was Big Sugar. Big Sugar (the large organizations that produce and use sugar in their products) have been manipulating and spinning data on sugar's health impacts for decades. Combine that with the fact that we are notoriously bad at maintaining the quality of digital data over time, and that digital data has grown explosively, and you have a challenging data environment in front of you when it comes to getting accurate information about sugar.

If we look at the Web as a living system, we could say that it is obese. While the tools, systems and processes for publishing and storing are abundant and cheap, the tools and processes for review and removal of what is out of date are anemic and weak. That's because we are addicted to publishing and we hate cleaning up after ourselves. If the Web was a digestive system, it would have no capacity to poop.

"The web made lots of content available for 'free'," medical journal editor, Susanna Guzman explains. "Whether it was good or reliable or not was of secondary concern, it seemed. As an editor working on the staff of a medical journal, I did everything I could to ensure that the journal's brand for being evidence-based and transparent was upheld. That publication, and others that stayed true to their brands and didn't sell out, are now benefiting from that decision. If they're still in business, that is. Many are not, having not been able to compete with free."

Digital bloat is everywhere. Going on the Web to find accurate information is an increasing challenge. Quality control is often very poor when it comes to Web content. Once it's up there, it's hardly ever reviewed. If new information emerges that makes what is already published out of date, misleading or wrong, there are rarely proper procedures in place to update, and where necessary remove, the out-of-date content.

That's surely not the case with health information, you say. Think again. I've worked with numerous health organizations over the years and their management of web content was patchy at best. At one stage, the US Department of Health had 200,000 pages on its website. It finally got around to reviewing what they had and deleted 150,000 of them. Nobody noticed. Not a single enquiry for one of those 150,000 pages. Why were they there? What purpose were these pages serving?

I have known other health organizations that hadn't reviewed their Web-based health information in five years or more. Here's the scary thing. In 25 years of working with organizations in 40 countries, I have found that in the majority of cases nobody is responsible for reviewing and removing out-of-date content. I have often pointed to out-of-date content. I would check again in another six months and the very same out-of-date content would still be there. When I stressed the need to keep the content up to date, the digital team would explain that management simply didn't care and would not provide enough resources for review. It was all publish, publish, publish.

It was thus with some trepidation that I decided to examine sugar-related health content. To create more focus, I decided to narrow my research to the potential relationship between sugar and cancer.

Sugar and cancer data

"There's a lot of confusing and misleading information on the Internet about the relationship between sugar and cancer," an article in Memorial Sloan Kettering stated in December 2016. "The notion that refined sugar causes cancer or that cutting sugar from the diet is a good way to treat cancer are two common—and incorrect—claims that turn up in a Google search." So, according to Sloan Kettering, it is incorrect to state that there is a connection between sugar and cancer. I decided to get in touch with Sloan Kettering about this blog post because I was finding lots of information on the Web indicating that there is a link between cancer and sugar. One such study, published in 2019, was even carried out by Sloan Kettering researchers.

Sloan Kettering were kind enough to reply, which was unusual because I got in touch with lots of organizations while doing this research and very few replied. This is not surprising. In my experience, most organizations are either unwilling or unable to respond to feedback. Once something gets published, it's finished. It might as well be set in stone. Reviewing it, responding to feedback on it, let alone taking it down, would be a truly exceptional activity. We must change that. We must make review and removal as important as publishing. This is how we will get control of the publishing flood and ensure quality, accurate information.

Sloan Kettering responded that what the blog post was trying to communicate was that there was not enough evidence of a direct link (causation) between sugar and cancer as and when it was written. However, they stated that they were "actively studying how sugar relates to cancer risk, treatment, and outcomes, so we certainly don't consider the possible link between sugar and cancer a 'myth'." What I concluded from my correspondence with Sloan Kettering is that while the link is not fully proven and more research needs to be done, there is enough evidence of a connection between sugar and cancer for further research.

Yet, as I looked at lots and lots of other sources from reputable organizations, I kept coming across the word "myth" in connection with sugar and cancer. For example, a Breastcancer.org page stated in 2019: "MYTH: Consuming too much sugar causes breast cancer. FACT: There is no evidence that sugar in the diet causes breast cancer."

A myth is a false belief or idea. A myth is the original fake news. Even in an age of zettabytes, words matter. When you say something is a myth you are using very strong, definitive language. In medicine, myths are associated with fraud, fallacies, fads, quacks. But is it really a myth that there is a link between sugar and breast cancer? A 2010 study by Universidade de Lisboa linked obesity and breast cancer, with sugar being a prime cause of obesity. "Epidemiological studies have shown that dietary sugar intake has a significant impact on the development of breast cancer," a 2016 study published by the National Center for Biotechnology Information stated. A study from Tufts University published in May 2019 linked excessive sugar intake to breast cancer.

Again and again, I kept coming across the word "myth." Again and again, I kept finding research that showed there was indeed a link between sugar and cancer. "A myth says: 'Sugar feeds cancer.' But the truth is that sugar doesn't make cancer grow faster," Cancer.org stated in October 2018. Cancer.org was kind enough to reply to me when I questioned the use of the word "myth." "Overall, there isn't enough good evidence to suggest that sugar itself can cause cancer or feed/help cancers," was their reply. "This doesn't mean that there aren't any studies which do suggest a link, but we base our advice on a review of all the available research and give more weight to the most rigorous scientific studies. We do try and highlight the indirect link between cancer risk and sugar. Eating lots of sugary foods over time can cause you to gain weight and there is strong evidence to show that being overweight or obese increases the risk of 13 different types of cancer."

That sort of reply is balanced, logical and reasonable. So why isn't that sort of balanced content published online? Why are so many eminent and respectable organizations still claiming that the sugar–cancer link is a myth? They're not stating that the link is unproven, that further evidence is required. They are instead stating that it is a myth, a fallacy. Is it simply because they have not updated their content? Perhaps.

Another reason may have to do with deeply embedded beliefs in nutritional science that have for the past 50 years downplayed the potential dangers of sugar as they pursued other theories and hypotheses for promoting healthy eating. Connected with that downplaying is an inevitable lack of research on the sugar–cancer link over the last 50 years because to do such research would have been frowned on by the medical establishment. It would not have been a good career move. Why? Because, behind the scenes, Big Sugar corporations have wielded huge power and influence over such research.

Data is political. There is always a story behind why certain data exists and why other data doesn't. Data is always imperfect because it reflects our imperfect society. Always be skeptical about data.

Corrupt data

"Can sugar cause cancer? It seems that evidence pointing this way was discovered in a study funded by the sugar industry nearly 50 years ago—but the work was never published," an article in Medical News Today stated in November 2017. Big Sugar, it seems, was repressing information that linked sugar to cancer and other diseases. For every set of Big Data, be sure there is a Big Sugar lurking in the background, spinning, lying, manipulating, hiding, distorting.

In 1972, John Yudkin, the founder of the Department of Nutrition at Queen Elizabeth College, London, stated that, "If only a small fraction of what we know about the effects of sugar were to be revealed in relation to any other material used as a food additive, that material would promptly be banned." On the other side of the Atlantic sat the king of US nutrition, US physiologist Ancel Keys. He relentlessly attacked Yudkin, calling his work "flimsy indeed," a "mountain of nonsense," "discredited propaganda." Keys and his cohorts silenced and discredited Yudkin. The message was very clear to up-and coming-nutritionists: If you want a career, don't touch sugar.

Some were brave, though. In 1976, Harvard nutritionist Jean Mayer linked sugar not just to tooth decay but also to obesity and diabetes. Big

Sugar immediately got to work, describing Mayer as a "scientific farce and a journalistic disgrace." According to Big Sugar, she was one of these "persuasive purveyors of nutritional rubbish," "opportunists dedicated to exploiting the consuming public." All who opposed Big Sugar were quacks.

In 2016, The New York Times reported that new evidence had emerged that in 1967 Big Sugar had paid three Harvard scientists to publish a review of research on sugar, fat and heart disease. The studies used in the review were handpicked by Big Sugar, and, of course, told a sweet story.

One of the scientists was Dr. Frederick Stare, then head of Harvard University's department of nutrition. Dr. Stare claimed that people got as much or more food value from processed foods as they did from natural food, which he called a "food fad." He advised people to eat "additives— they're good for you." He thought that Coca-Cola was a wonderful "healthy between-meals snack." He loved sugar, calling it "a quick energy boon and pleasant to take." You guessed it. Big Sugar was pumping donations into his department.

Another scientist who wrote the Big Sugar article was Mark Hegsted, who would go on to draft the forerunner to the US federal government's dietary guidelines. In 1980, the US issued its first set of dietary guidelines. 15% of US citizens were obese when these guidelines were published. By 2016, it was 40%. Correlation is not causation, though it is a bit strange that after the first dietary guidelines were published, US obesity bulged. The committee writing the 2020 US nutrition guidelines was well sprinkled with former lobbyists and those who have been funded by Big Sugar and Big Food.

Bias in data is rampant, as we will see in the chapter on artificial intelligence. Many organizations are either unable or unwilling to ensure that their data is fair and objective. If you use dodgy, corrupt data, you get dodgy, corrupt results. Personalizing crap data gives you personalized crap.

More data, less light

One of the reasons organizations may give for claiming something is a myth when in fact the reality is more complex and subtle, is that they need to make things simple, to "dumb down" for the general public. There is some merit to this argument. Another reason is that many organizations have still not adapted to how the Web has changed communications, from a one-way, controlled channel to a messy mix of diverse publishing and feedback. Historically, such organizations were often the only source of information on the subject within a country.

There is also a culture in traditional publishing that believes that that which is published is to be revered and that what has gone before sets the scene for the future. If your organization has been calling something a myth for decades, it's hard to change the language, the tone. As well, organizations everywhere are notoriously bad at being able to review, update and where appropriate remove or archive. Review and maintenance are so essential when it comes to data. We must become much better at taking care of what we have rather than constantly creating new stuff.

A counter-argument is that we should allow everything to be published. That the flood of new data will ultimately drive science and society forward. If we look back in history to other revolutions in communication, we find that this was not always the case. With information comes misinformation. We see how in the United States and Great Britain, for example, Facebook et al. are accelerating the development of misinformation societies.

"There is no evidence that, except in religion, printing hastened the spread of new ideas... In fact, the printing of medieval scientific texts may have delayed the acceptance of Copernicus," Elizabeth Eisenstein wrote in her book, The Printing Revolution in Early Modern Europe.

We must manage our data much better. We must establish processes to root out as much as possible of what is wrong, what has been deliberately manipulated, what is prejudicial, what is fake. Otherwise, the digital world—whose building blocks are data—will become a world of crap and lies.

Back around 2011, the Norwegian Cancer Society had a 5,000-page website, with 45 part-time publishers. The Society carried out a Top Tasks survey, which is a research method I developed to help understand what really matters to people. The results showed that a very small set of tasks, centering around treatment, symptoms and diagnosis, were vastly more important to people than a whole range of other content. A comprehensive review of the content on the website began. Lots of duplicate content was discovered. This was mainly because the Society worked in departmental silos, each silo creating its own content, unaware that similar content existed in another silo.

It was found that having 45 part-time publishers was unmanageable and ineffective. Because publishing content was a small part of these people's jobs, they could never find time to properly review, to collaborate with others who were publishing, or to do training and improve their skills. It was decided that the team should be reduced to six people who would be able to dedicate a substantial portion of their time to content. These people would also actively collaborate with each other.

The result was that the site was reduced from 5,000 to 500 pages that were consistently reviewed and managed. The Society is a charity and needs to get donations from the public. On the old site, there were calls for donations everywhere. However, the Top Tasks results clearly showed that donating to the Society was in no way a top task. A brave decision was made to focus on the citizens' top tasks of treatment, symptoms and prevention, and to remove lots of content connected with donations. The results? Nurses reported that when interacting with people who had been to the website, they were clearly better informed. And donations? Donations doubled.

During the Ebola crisis, the Ebola factsheet page on the World Health Organization (WHO) website was a vital resource for doctors, nurses and other interested parties. Yet it was a real challenge to get this page reviewed and updated. The reason was that the WHO was so focused on publishing new information about Ebola that it struggled to review and update essential content that was already published. It seemed that everybody within the WHO wanted to publish something on Ebola, to show what they or their division was doing to combat the disease. The WHO knew how important the factsheet page was, how it was infinitely more important than the vast majority of other pages on Ebola, but it too was paralyzed by a tsunami of internal publishing.

The Web is great. All the challenges data faces can be overcome. Let me tell you a story about a fellow named Tom. It was 1993 and Tom was living in Washington DC. Tom had a serious hip issue. He was aware of research about a novel approach to hip surgery and he was constantly asking his doctor to get him a copy of the research. After months and months of trying to get his doctor to give him the research, Tom got frustrated and went to a medical library. There, he was arrested for attempting to get the research. Arrested.

A Web full of data, for all its drawbacks, is infinitely better than a world where some high priests guard the knowledge. We must learn to navigate the data, to filter and interpret it. If we create data and information, we must take responsibility for it, from the day it's published until the day it's removed—should that day need to arrive. We must review what we publish with a regularity that reflects its likelihood to go out of date.

Key actions

Make continuous review central to all publishing activities. Only publish the content you have the capacity to professionally manage on an ongoing basis. Review means re-editing where appropriate and removing where necessary.

Links

The sugar conspiracy, Ian Leslie, The Guardian, 2016
https://www.theguardian.com/society/2016/apr/07/the-sugar-conspiracy-robert-lustig-john-yudkin

A former corn-syrup lobbyist is drafting new federal dietary rules (seriously), David Lazarus, LA Times, 2019
https://www.latimes.com/business/lazarus/la-fi-lazarus-food-industry-shapes-dietary-guidelines-20190507-story.html

An Evolutionary Explanation For Why We Crave Sugar, Dina Spector, Business Insider, 2014,
https://www.businessinsider.com/evolutionary-reason-we-love-sugar-2014-4?r=US&IR=T

The Shady History of Big Sugar, David Singerman, New York Times, 2016
https://www.nytimes.com/2016/09/17/opinion/the-shady-history-of-big-sugar.html

How the Sugar Industry Shifted Blame to Fat, Anahad O'Connor, New York Times, 2016
https://www.nytimes.com/2016/09/13/well/eat/how-the-sugar-industry-shifted-blame-to-fat.html

Sugar Industry and Coronary Heart Disease Research, JAMA Network, 2016
https://jamanetwork.com/journals/jamainternalmedicine/article-abstract/2548255

7 Reasons why sugar is called 'The White Death', Times of India, 2017
https://recipes.timesofindia.com/articles/food-facts/7-reasons-why-sugar-is-called-the-white-death/photostory/60388518.cms?picid=60388567

The Case Against Sugar, Gary Taubes, Granta Publications, 2016
https://www.goodreads.com/book/show/29874881-the-case-against-sugar

Sugar: The world corrupted, from slavery to obesity, James Walvin, Pegasus Books, 2018
https://www.goodreads.com/en/book/show/35407604-sugar

Humans have bred fruits to be so sweet, a zoo had to stop feeding them to some animals, Katherine Ellen Foley, QUARTZ, 2018
https://qz.com/1408469/humans-have-bred-fruits-to-be-so-high-in-sugar-a-zoo-had-to-stop-feeding-them-to-some-animals/

A history of sugar – the food nobody needs, but everyone craves, M. Horton, A. Bentley, P. Langton, The Conversation, 2015
https://theconversation.com/a-history-of-sugar-the-food-nobody-needs-but-everyone-craves-49823

Child labour, poverty and terrible working conditions lie behind the sugar you eat, Nicki Lisa Cole, The Conversation, 2018
https://theconversation.com/child-labour-poverty-and-terrible-working-conditions-lie-behind-the-sugar-you-eat-95242

Adult obesity: Is childhood sugar intake in the '70s to blame? Ana Sandoiu, Medical News Today, 2019
https://www.medicalnewstoday.com/articles/326449.php#1

Exploding plastic inevitable

Andy's dream

"I want to be plastic," Andy Warhol said. Warhol loved plastic so much that in 1966 he called his new show the Exploding Plastic Inevitable, because at that stage plastic had become part of the fabric of modern life.

Andy's dream is coming true. Fish, animals, birds, and humans are ingesting plastic daily. We are eating and drinking microplastic and breathing in nanoplastic. (A microplastic is a very small piece of plastic pollutant that is less than 5 mm in length. A nanoplastic is typically less than 100 nanometers in size; a human hair has a diameter of about 75,000 nanometers.)

Plastic has become so common that geologists are noticing the emergence of a sedimentary layer of plastic. This is how "modern" humans will be remembered. We turned the world into plastic. All for our own convenience. All because we wouldn't clean up after ourselves. All because it was so cheap it was irresistible. And we did it, historically speaking, in the blink of an eye.

In wasn't until the 1940s that plastic truly bloomed, though its roots go back a bit further. Ironically, environmentalism was one of the motivations for the creation of plastic. In late nineteenth-century USA, the game of billiards was very popular. Billiard balls were at that time made from ivory, resulting in the slaughter of a huge number of elephants. The invention of the first plastic billiard ball wasn't a great success, though. The celluloid was volatile, and when two billiard balls cracked together, a small explosion (like a gunshot) often occurred, which didn't go down well in Western saloons. (The plastic bag was another response to the environment, invented to save trees.)

Plastic is so cheap to create because it is usually made from the waste material from oil production. It's much cheaper to manufacture a finished plastic product than it is to make a steel or wooden one. This is because of plastic's malleability. Pour some hot plastic into a mold and out pops a plastic part. Plastic bags, for example, require very little energy and raw materials. It takes three times the energy to create an equivalent paper bag and 131 times the energy to create a similar-size cotton one.

As the 20th century progressed, more and more types of plastic were developed. It wasn't just Warhol who thought of plastic as a wonder product. Chemists dreamt of "Plastic Man" who would "come into a world of color and bright shining surfaces... a world in which man, like a magician, makes what he wants for almost every need," British chemists Victor Yarsley and Edward Couzens wrote. Plastic Man would grow up "surrounded by unbreakable toys, rounded corners, unscuffable walls, warpless windows, dirt-proof fabrics, and lightweight cars and planes and boats." In old age, he would wear plastic glasses and plastic dentures, and when he died, he would be "hygienically enclosed in a plastic coffin."

The magic of plastic was the magic of innovation, invention, modernity and convenience, at a price that was so cheap it was irresistible. Promoting the benefits of throwaway plastic, House Beautiful magazine assured readers in 1953 that, "You will have a greater chance to be yourself than any people in the history of civilization."

Again and again, we are told that our products, whether they be plastic chairs or smartphones, will allow us to be more ourselves. There is truth in that, though it's not the whole truth. First, we make the tool, then the tool makes us. We must stop our products making us. We must resist the call of the new. We are made of better stuff than to be defined by what we buy.

Plastic trained us well. We learned to throw away rather than to pick up, to discard rather than to repair. We weren't always so wasteful. "In the US, prior to 1950, reusable packaging such as glass bottles had a nearly 96% return rate," Stephen Buranyi wrote for The Guardian. By the 1970s, it had dropped to a 5% return rate. If we once were able to reuse and return things, then we have the capacity to change back to those more environmentally friendly ways.

Plastic production began to take off with the advent of the Second World War, with US plastic production tripling between 1939 and 1945. But that was just a taste of what was to come. In 1950, worldwide production of plastics was two million tons. By 2017, it was 400 million tons. It's estimated that there are now more than eight billion tons of plastic, with over 80% of it dumped as waste. As with data, most of the plastic that exists today has been made in the last decade and it's predicted that plastic production will double by 2035.

Oceans of waste

A lot of this plastic ends up in the oceans, where it often gathers as enormous garbage patches, the largest of which is three times the size of France. Plastic is pretty much impossible to get rid of, but it does break down over time, into microplastics and nanoplastics.

"To sea turtles, plastic bags in the water can look like jellyfish, floating on the surface plastic can appear to be a tasty snack for a seagull, and to baby perch it appears more appetizing than the plankton they are supposed to eat," Ian Johnston wrote for The Independent. Plastic nurdles are particularly damaging to ocean life. These pellets of plastic are the raw materials from which plastic goods are made. "It isn't hard to see why birds mistake them for fish eggs and gulp them down," Michael Lucy wrote for Cosmos.

Research published by the Scripps Institution of Oceanography in 2019 estimated that our oceans could hold a million times more plastic than previously estimated. A 2016 Ellen MacArthur Foundation report estimated that by 2050 the weight of plastic in the oceans will be greater than the weight of fish. In San Francisco, it's estimated that rainfall washes more than seven trillion microplastics off the streets and into San Francisco Bay each year.

A study by University of Newcastle, Australia, estimated that we could be ingesting a credit card's worth of plastic every week. Another study by King's College London, found London air contained so much plastic that each day from 575 to 1,008 pieces of plastic fell to the ground per square meter, with 15 different plastics identified. Microplastics and nanoplastics are magnets for toxins, which wrap around the plastics, only to separate when ingested by fish, birds and humans. Once loosed from the plastic, the toxins migrate to the flesh and organs.

There is no place on Earth you can escape plastic waste. There is no "away" where you can throw plastic. It will always land, sink, float or rise somewhere. Mount Everest is littered with plastic. The Mariana Trench, the deepest part of the ocean, is home to plastic waste. The most isolated, uninhabited Pacific islands are inundated with plastic waste.

Plastic is in practically everything. You wouldn't think teabags are made from plastic. A study found that a single teabag at brewing temperature "released about 11.6 billion microplastic and 3.1 billion nanoplastic particles into the water." About 50% of a new car or plane is made up of plastic. A typical computer can be up to 40% plastic. It's estimated that 336,000 metric tons of plastic were used in the manufacture of cell phones in 2017, up from 282,000 metric tons in 2013. Most clothes contain significant quantities of plastic, as we'll see in the next chapter. Every year about 250,000 single-use tents are left behind at UK music festivals. These tents cost about £25. Why would anyone bother recycling or hanging on to them?

The recycling con

Plastic recycling has always been much more a PR stunt than a reality. Of all the plastic produced, only about 10% has been recycled. Even the plastic you can recycle degrades every time you recycle it. You can recycle glass and steel almost endlessly and still get the same quality, but not plastic.

In the 1970s, there were serious moves to curtail the use of plastic. Big Plastic used the "Guns don't kill people" defense to tremendous effect. Through clever messaging, they managed to blame the consumer. Plastic doesn't kill people. Instead, the sloth and laziness of ordinary people is the root cause of the problem. Whatever you do, don't blame industry. We just produce the plastic. The spinmeisters promoted recycling and personal responsibility and won the day.

We can't contain the menacing flood of plastic, we are told, because of the jobs, because of our growth-at-all-costs culture, because of the sheer convenience that plastic brings to our lives. To uproot plastic is to change the economy. To change the economy we must first change the universal human culture that prizes convenience, cheap stuff and more stuff over the long-term sustainability of life on this planet.

We must move from a culture where the human is primary and all Earth is there for our consumption and convenience, to one where humans are part of the Earth, part of nature, and where we all need to play a part for the health and happiness and long-term survival of the whole.

But plastic does good, we hear. Plastic keeps those vegetables and fruits fresh and allows us to import our exotic desires from great distances. Selling grapes in sealed trays versus in loose bunches can save as much as 20% in waste, we are told. Our costing models are flawed. We calculate everything based on the near-term and so little on the long-term.

The greater the speed we move at, the more we become short-term thinkers. We see the rotting fruit as a loss to the supermarket. We don't see the plastic waste that never rots as a loss for our planet and everything on it. But plastic still has a role to play, they say. Plastic packaging is lighter, cheaper and stronger than other packaging materials. The answer is not alternative packaging. The answer is radically less packaging. Bring our own bags, collect stuff, receive stuff in reusable packages and give those back. Less convenient for sure. We can do this. The effort is so worth it.

We have created an economics that gives to the present by taking from the future. We calculate short-term, immediate costs. What is the total lifetime cost of a piece of plastic, a smartphone, or a digital image? Who pays to clean up the seas and the data lakes?

No packaging

Loop is a company that creates high-quality, reusable packaging for foodstuffs. A variety of food products are delivered to the home, then when used, the containers are sent back and cleaned and used again. This sort of circular economy thinking is vital.

I have been told about a Belgian farming initiative whereby every year the farmers and local families invest together in the coming year's crop. In return, families will receive a weekly basket of produce. This model supports local farming by providing upfront capital and risk sharing. (If some of the crops fail, the families accept that they will get less.) Packaging is greatly reduced because all the produce is delivered in one reusable basket. Key to reducing packaging is going local; the closer we are to the source of the product, the less packaging will be required.

It's not too late for us to change, though, as Bob Dylan sang, "it's getting there." In recent years, the public have truly awakened to the dangers of plastic. Some countries have started taxing plastic bags. African countries such as Tanzania, Kenya and Rwanda are leading the way when it comes to banning plastic. There is progress. We need a lot more.

Key actions

Avoid plastic packaging. Bring your own bag and avoid the barcodes. Whenever you can replace plastic with another material, do, but don't replace it simply for the sake of it. If you have a plastic bag, use the hell out of it.

Links

The simple idea that could be the answer to our plastic problem: reusable packaging, Joel Makower, World Economic Forum, 2019
https://www.weforum.org/agenda/2019/01/loop-s-launch-brings-reusable-packaging-to-the-world-s-biggest-brands

The plastic backlash: what's behind our sudden rage – and will it make a difference? Stephen Buranyi, The Guardian, 2018
https://www.theguardian.com/environment/2018/nov/13/the-plastic-backlash-whats-behind-our-sudden-rage-and-will-it-make-a-difference

Some plastic with your tea? Nathalie Tufenkji, McGill, 2019
https://www.mcgill.ca/newsroom/channels/news/some-plastic-your-tea-300919

Greenpeace: And our survey says…Ban the bead! Greenpeace, 2016
https://storage.googleapis.com/gpuk-old-wp-site/and-our-survey-saysban-bead-20160414/index.html

A bold plan to ban single-use plastic in nation of 1.3 billion has been shelved, Manveena Suri, CNN, 2019
https://edition.cnn.com/2019/10/03/india/modi-india-plastic-ban-intl-hnk-scli/index.html

Production, use, and fate of all plastics ever made, R. Geyer, J. Jambeck, K. Lavender Law, Science Advances, 2017
https://advances.sciencemag.org/content/3/7/e1700782

How plastic is damaging planet Earth, Ian Johnston, The Independent, 2017
https://www.independent.co.uk/environment/plastic-how-planet-Earth-environment-oceans-wildlife-recycling-landfill-artificial-a7972226.html

Ending the age of plastic, Michael Lucy, Cosmos, 2018
https://cosmosmagazine.com/geoscience/ending-the-age-of-plastic

The ocean is teeming with microplastic – a million times more than we thought, suggests new research, Johnny Wood, World Economic Forum, 2019
https://www.weforum.org/agenda/2019/12/microplastics-ocean-plastic-pollution-research-salps

Will there be more fish or plastic in the sea in 2050? Leo Hornak, BBC, 2016
https://www.bbc.com/news/magazine-35562253

'Throwaway Living': When Tossing Out Everything Was All the Rage, Ben Cosgrove, TIME, 2014
https://time.com/3879873/throwaway-living-when-tossing-it-all-was-all-the-rage/

Plastic fantastic: How it changed the world, Robert Plummer, BBC, 2018
https://www.bbc.com/news/business-42646025

The biggest likely source of microplastics in California coastal waters? Our car tires, Rosanna Xia, LA Times, 2019
https://www.latimes.com/environment/story/2019-10-02/california-microplastics-ocean-study

A Brief History of Plastic's Conquest of the World, Susan Freinkel, Scientific American, 2011
https://www.scientificamerican.com/article/a-brief-history-of-plastic-world-conquest/

The environmental cost of dumping your tent at the Electric Picnic, Aurore Julien, RTE, 2019
https://www.rte.ie/brainstorm/2019/0822/1070274-the-environmental-cost-of-dumping-your-tent-at-electric-picnic/

Fossil fuel industry sees the future in hard-to-recycle plastic, Deirdre McKay, The Conversation, 2019
https://theconversation.com/fossil-fuel-industry-sees-the-future-in-hard-to-recycle-plastic-123631

War on plastic waste faces setback as cost of recycled material soars, Jillian Ambrose, The Guardian, 2019
https://www.theguardian.com/environment/2019/oct/13/war-on-plastic-waste-faces-setback-as-cost-of-recycled-material-soars

'Sustainable' Lego: Why plastics from plants won't solve the pollution crisis, Sharon George, Deirdre McKay, The Independent, 2018
https://www.independent.co.uk/news/science/sustainable-lego-plastic-plants-pollution-crisis-a8266256.html

Plastic packaging problem: Five innovative ideas, Katharine Rooney, World Economic Forum, 2019
https://www.weforum.org/agenda/2019/10/plastic-packaging-environment-design-loop

The battle to break plastic's bonds, Victoria Gill, BBC, 2019
https://www.bbc.com/news/science-environment-50143451

Africa is leading the world in plastic bag bans, Ephrat Livni, World Economic Forum, 2019
https://www.weforum.org/agenda/2019/05/africa-is-leading-the-world-in-plastic-bag-bans

You eat a credit card's worth of plastic a week, research says, Emma Charlton, World Economic Forum, 2019
https://www.weforum.org/agenda/2019/06/you-eat-a-credit-card-s-worth-of-plastic-a-week-research-says

London study: microplastic pollution is raining down on city dwellers, Damian Carrington, The Guardian, 2019
https://www.theguardian.com/environment/2019/dec/27/revealed-microplastic-pollution-is-raining-down-on-city-dwellers

Things You Didn't Know About Plastic (and Recycling), Lilly Sedaghat, National Geographic, 2018
https://blog.nationalgeographic.org/2018/04/04/7-things-you-didnt-know-about-plastic-and-recycling/

Fashionwaste

Toxic style

Fast Fashion could not have the same corrosive impact without digital. Instagram Culture is ravenous for the new, for the fast, for the flashy, for the fake. The reason why a design idea can be turned into an actual product within days is primarily down to digital accelerants. Digital has the world on speed, turning fashion's seasons into a frenzied blur of continuous releases. These ultra-cheap, disposable items have a business model based on selling large volumes of low-quality, eye-catching clothes at slim margins.

What this means is that those at the bottom of the production chain (mainly female workers) work as little more than slave labor in order to meet our fleeting whims. They are ground down by grueling 12-hour-plus days in horrible conditions to produce clothes that we throw away without a thought. These practices always existed but the slave-driving, ramped-up, frenzied speed could never have been possible without MacBooks, iPhones, Adobe, logistics software, the Cloud, and all that digital jazz.

Digital makes humans work faster than is good for our wellbeing. Why? To get stuff done faster. Why? Because everyone wants stuff fast these days? Why? Because it's so important to be new and up to date? Why?

The history of textiles is interlinked with the history of sugar. If African slaves were not being brutalized under the Brazilian or Caribbean sun to cut sugar cane, they were being brutalized in the United States to pick cotton. Just as the raw sugar was sent to England and Portugal to be processed, so the raw cotton was sent to England to be spun. Finished product was then often sold on to countries like India, undermining and destroying native industries. Nothing much has changed. Fast Fashion creates slave-like conditions and undermines and destroys native fashion industries.

Fast Fashion pollution is increasingly plastic. Polyester, nylon, acrylic, and other plastic fibers make up about 60% of the material used to make most modern clothes. Plastic is cheap, versatile and convenient. It stretches and breathes and can be warm and cool where required. The vibrant colors and fabric finishes are usually achieved through the liberal application of chemicals, making textile dyeing one of the biggest global polluters of water.

"Sulphur, naphthol, vat dyes, nitrates, acetic acid, soaps, enzymes, chromium compounds and heavy metals like copper, arsenic, lead, cadmium, mercury, nickel, and cobalt and certain auxiliary chemicals all collectively make the textile effluent highly toxic," Rita Kant, assistant professor at Panjab University, India explains.

Fast Fashion is a truly globalized industry, highly dependent on the Internet and other networks. Where the clothes are made is rarely where they're sold. To get its disposable items to the marketplace, massive container ships are used. These lumbering colossuses burn gigantic amounts of the lowest-grade, filthiest fuel imaginable—1,000 times dirtier than truck diesel. According to a 2018 report by Quantis, an environmental consultancy, the global apparel and footwear industries annually emit nearly four metric gigatons of pollution, almost as much as the entire European Union.

We'd need to plant 400 billion trees to offset that sort of pollution. That's 80 times more trees than are currently being planted in a year. Actually, it's much worse. As they rot, clothes emit methane, which is 30 times worse for global warming than CO_2. Thus, we would need to plant 12 trillion trees to deal with Fast Fashion pollution, which happens to be four times more trees than currently exist on Earth. We must consume much less or else we will bestow a wasteland to our children and grandchildren.

In Europe, fashion houses began to develop in the nineteenth century, with France leading the way. Until quite recently, there were two fashion seasons or collections: Spring/Summer, Fall/Winter. Fast Fashion and digital changed all that. By 2011, there were an average of five collections, and by 2019, Fast Fashion creators like Zara had 24 collections a year.

Clothing production doubled from 2000 to 2014. The average consumer bought 60% more garments in 2014 than at the beginning of the decade, while wearing them for half as long, with many having at least two items in their wardrobe that they had never worn. In the UK alone, more than two tons of clothes are bought every minute, with each ton producing 23.3 tons of CO_2. We'd need to be planting 2,300 trees per minute for a year to deal with that pollution. (That's 1.2 billion trees in a year.)

Globally, every second, the equivalent of an entire garbage truck full of textiles is dumped or burned. Every second. Not every minute, not every hour—every second. Nearly 60% of all clothing is dumped or incinerated within a year of being produced. Most of it is dumped; the plastic living forever, with the stewing mess of chemical goo releasing methane.

It's estimated that as much as 20% of a fabric may be discarded during the manufacturing process. Excess inventory is another issue. Companies are known to incinerate unsold clothes to protect the "integrity" of the brand, like Burberry did in 2018 when it burned $37 million worth of new clothing and cosmetics to maintain its "brand value."

Fast Fashion finds humanity at its most obscene, wasteful worst, dressed in the riches of ruins. Try explaining to an alien how a brand manufactures a new pair of jeans and then goes to the extra cost and effort to send it through another process to tear it in order to make it look "old" and "worn." The alien would think you're crazy. Humans. We're crazy.

Fast Fashion clothes shed micro- and nanofibers. Like skin is always shedding dead scales, every time you put on these clothes, every time you walk down a corridor or street, your clothes are shedding thousands and thousands of micro- and nanofibers, some of which you breathe in. (Gives a new meaning to the term "breathable clothing.")

It gets worse when you wash them. A single load of laundry can release hundreds of thousands of plastic fibers into the water supply. These fibers are so small that there aren't any washing machine filters that can catch them. The more water used, the more fibers released, so delicate wash cycles are the most polluting.

Using lots of natural materials is not the answer. Cotton is very popular, but it is a highly water-intensive plant. Also, even though only 2.4% of the world's agricultural land is planted with cotton, 10% of all agricultural chemicals and 25% of pesticides are used in cotton production.

Poor work

Of the clothes that are reused or recycled, it is estimated that up to 90% of them are exported to poorer countries, collapsing native fashion industries and/or overloading poorly regulated dumps. "This act of exporting charity clothing to struggling nations [has] turned into a multi-billion-dollar industry, which targets and makes victims of some of the world's poorest countries, forcing them deeper into the cycle of poverty and further away from any type of development, freedom and identity within their own fashion industry," journalist Ola Onikoyi writes.

Millions of poor Bangladeshi and Vietnamese women are paid a couple of dollars to work all day for Fast Fashion's throwaway style. Working in horrible conditions in factories prone to collapse and fire. At least we're giving them a job, the logic goes, even if the job pays so poorly that their children at home are often starving because their mothers don't earn enough to put enough food on the table. Fast Fashion is in a spiraling race to the bottom, with prices always under pressure, and a mad rush for flexibility. The convenience of the fickle customer trumps everything. These promises of speed, these promises of convenience, they come at a cost, a cost the poorest workers pay. A cost the Earth pays.

Fast Fashion is a part of fast commerce, like what Amazon practices, where the pressure on the workers at the lowest level is unrelenting. Digital makes you work faster. If you're a warehouse worker, it tracks your every second, monitoring and measuring, setting limb-busting targets. Where you find Amazon or Uber workers, you will find pee bottles hidden somewhere because they don't have the time to go to the toilet. Exhaustion and injuries abound. (In the US, Amazon workers are twice as likely to get injured as the national average.) Our convenience trumps worker rights.

Convenience trumps health. The US—the digital homeland—is the only "modern" country where life expectancy is dropping, as millions die of preventable illnesses. "Mortality from deaths of despair far surpasses anything seen in America since the dawn of the 20th century," a US Congress committee stated in 2019. This is the house Facebook and Google built. This is the house Fast Fashion built. This is the house Amazon built, that Apple and Microsoft built. After 50 years or more of digital "innovation," where is the better society?

This is the cliff convenience, efficiency and speed are driving us off. We need to slow down and think a lot more. The fashion designers on their MacBooks in Stockholm, London, New York, Paris or Barcelona, who have thought up the latest fashion that is actually a copy of the latest fashion two years ago that was a copy of the latest fashion four years ago, because when you've got 24 collections a year and you're under intense pressure to deliver, everything begins to blur into everything else, yes, they will not suffer as much as the poor factory worker when the demand is made that their latest copy, fake, Fast Fashion gets made in ultrafast time.

Rather, it will be the poor woman in some far-off place who cannot get home this weekend—even though she hasn't been home in months—to see her children because her boss has told her that she must work overtime and she will be fired if she doesn't because there's always someone poorer, someone more desperate. It will be the poor worker in some Amazon-like warehouse driven to despair and exhaustion, peeing in a plastic bottle, under the hammer of robot-time, as they rush to pack another pair of torn jeans into another plastic and cardboard box made from trees that didn't need to be cut down so that someone somewhere will have another item in their wardrobe that they will never even wear or will return because they've changed their mind about the color.

And yet the designers do feel the whiplash of Fast Fashion too. It is surely not the dream of a young fashion designer to exploit poor workers, encourage disposability and fill dumps with toxic waste, and work in a relentless blur of busyness. As the nature of digital adds more and more speed to Fast Fashion—and to every other industry—the designers are being ground down and burnt out too, not as cruelly as the factory workers—but strung out on speed they surely are. Why?

Buy fewer clothes, pay more for them, wear them until they are genuinely worn and with holes in them, and if you don't like the holes, get them mended. Make genuinely old and worn a style, not fake new clothes that try to look old. Wash only when necessary.

Taking more individual responsibility is good but it is not nearly enough. The big brands are the root cause of the Fast Fashion epidemic. If they were forced to take back and reuse their clothes once the consumer had finished wearing them, then we would see real change. These brands have the most sophisticated digitally-driven processes imaginable when it comes to the making and the marketing of their products, but when it comes to the paltry initiatives for recycling and reuse, that's still all done by hand, a slow manual process that has no possible hope of dealing with the masses of waste that Fast Fashion churns out every day. Big Fashion has grown rich by impoverishing the Earth. We must force the brands to turn their waste into raw materials. Then, real change will occur.

Go to the effort of finding local brands that have sustainable models. Here, the Web can help. Reader Ernst Décsey told me of how he bought a dress for his wife from a local brand, hopaal.fr, which he discovered through search. The dress was made from 100% recycled materials. They also offered delivery with a re-usable packaging option from originalrepack.com.

Key actions

Boycott the big brands. Buy local. Repair local. Wear the hell out of your clothes and proudly show off your real patches and real tears.

Links

More than ever, our clothes are made of plastic. Just washing them can pollute the oceans, Brian Resnick, Vox, 2019
https://www.vox.com/the-goods/2018/9/19/17800654/clothes-plastic-pollution-polyester-washing-machine

Vicious cycle: delicate wash releases more plastic microfibres, Ian Sample, The Guardian, 2019
https://www.theguardian.com/environment/2019/sep/26/vicious-cycle-delicate-wash-releases-more-plastic-microfibres

A more potent greenhouse gas than CO2, methane emissions will leap as Earth warms, Morgan Kelly, Princeton, 2014
https://blogs.princeton.edu/research/2014/03/26/a-more-potent-greenhouse-gas-than-co2-methane-emissions-will-leap-as-Earth-warms-nature/

The environmental costs of fast fashion, Patsy Perry, The Independent, 2018
https://www.independent.co.uk/life-style/fashion/environment-costs-fast-fashion-pollution-waste-sustainability-a8139386.html

The True Cost: documentary on the downsides of the Fast Fashion industry, 2015
https://truecostmovie.com/

The ugly side of fast fashion: This is the scary impact it's having on our world, Geraldine Carton, Image, 2019
https://www.image.ie/life/ugly-fast-fashion-scary-impact-world-environment-142426

Who's Really Paying for Our Cheap Clothes? Lorraine Chow, EcoWatch, 2015
https://www.ecowatch.com/whos-really-paying-for-our-cheap-clothes-1882033894.html

Textile dyeing industry an environmental hazard, Rita Kant, Scientific Research, 2012
http://file.scirp.org/Html/4-8301582_17027.htm

One garbage truck of textiles wasted every second: report creates vision for change, Ellen MacArthur Foundation, 2017
https://www.ellenmacarthurfoundation.org/news/one-garbage-truck-of-textiles-wasted-every-second-report-creates-vision-for-change

Charity Clothes—A Bane of the African fashion Industry, Ola Onikoyi, Medium, 2019
https://medium.com/@olaonikoyi/charity-clothes-a-bane-of-the-african-fashion-industry-and-a-call-on-the-afcfta-8cd3d75e6b59

Fast fashion produces more carbon emissions per minute than driving a car around the world six times, Oxfam, 2019
https://oxfamapps.org/media/press_release/fast-fashion-produces-more-carbon-emissions-per-minute-than-driving-a-car-around-the-world-six-times-oxfam/

Long-Term Trends in Deaths of Despair, United States Congress, 2019
https://www.jec.senate.gov/public/index.cfm/republicans/2019/9/long-term-trends-in-deaths-of-despair

Time to make fast fashion a problem for its makers, not charities, Mark Liu, PHYS.org, 2019
https://phys.org/news/2019-09-fast-fashion-problem-makers-charities.html

Style that's sustainable: A new fast-fashion formula, N. Remy, E. Speelman, S. Swartz, McKinsey, 2016
https://www.mckinsey.com/business-functions/sustainability/our-insights/style-thats-sustainable-a-new-fast-fashion-formula

Environmental impact of the textile and clothing industry, Nikolina Šajn, European Parliament, 2019
https://www.europarl.europa.eu/RegData/etudes/BRIE/2019/633143/EPRS_BRI(2019)633143_EN.pdf

How polluting is the fashion industry? Cameron Boggon, EKOenergy, 2019
https://www.ekoenergy.org/how-polluting-is-the-fashion-industry/

The high cost of fast fashion, Alacoque McAlpine, RTE, 2019
https://www.rte.ie/brainstorm/2018/0321/948976-the-high-cost-of-fast-fashion/

Slow Fashion 101, Kyle Kowalski, SLOWW
https://www.sloww.co/slow-fashion-101/

Can Recycled Rags Fix Fashion's Waste Problem? Winston Choi-Schagrin, New York Times, 2019
https://www.nytimes.com/2019/12/21/fashion/fabscrap-fashion-waste-recycyling.html?smid=nytcore-ios-share

Cotton on: the staggering potential of switching to organic clothes, Rebecca Smithers, The Guardian, 2019
https://www.theguardian.com/fashion/2019/oct/01/cotton-on-the-staggering-potential-of-switching-to-organic-clothes

Ruthless Quotas at Amazon Are Maiming Employees, Will Evans, The Atlantic, 2019
https://www.theatlantic.com/technology/archive/2019/11/amazon-warehouse-reports-show-worker-injuries/602530/

Phonewaste

10 billion smartphones

I love my smartphone. It's indispensable to the life I want to lead. I grew up on a small farm, communing with the silence and commuting with the cows as we walked slowly from the upper fields to the milking shed. It sucked. I hated it. I remember the first time I saw the Web in the early 1990s. It was a magical experience. I still think the Web, for all its drawbacks, is an extraordinarily wonderful place. Smartphones are a modern wonder. I couldn't and wouldn't live without one.

The first smartphone was produced in 2007. By 2019, about 10 billion had been made. Every year, about 1.5 billion new smartphones are sold. Manufacturing a smartphone can produce as much as 90% of the pollution it creates during its lifetime, according to a study from McMaster University in Canada. That means that you should try and hold on to your phone for at least five years, because by far the biggest environmental cost is in its manufacture. However, on average, people tend to hold on to their phones for only two to three years.

"Always at the cutting edge," an ad for Deutsche Telekom stated. It promised that "customers will never miss another innovation," because of a new plan that allowed a change of phone every twelve months. With fabulous deals like this, it's not surprising that by 2014 there were more than 100 million phones lying unused and unrecycled in the drawers of German households, which is a drop in the bucket of the estimated old and unused smartphones out there. Perfectly good phones that had a massive pollution cost to produce are lying around unused and unrecycled. Into these smartphones we demanded from the Earth 100 units of energy and resources. After we've used up the equivalent of 20 units, we discard the thing, leaving 80 units of unused energy, which becomes waste.

I'm as guilty as anyone. I've never changed a phone because it was broken or worn. I was on a plan and when the plan said I could have a new phone, I jumped and bought my new phone like the good little consumer I'd been trained to be. It was a treat, a sugar rush. If we could only reduce the waste, we'd do so much good in the world, and we'd live less stressful, more fulfilled lives.

The energy that is consumed by a smartphone when it is running is relatively little. However, a key reason that smartphones don't consume so much running energy themselves is because they get data centers to do a lot of the energy-intensive heavy-lifting processing for them. What this means, of course, is that data center and network growth must go hand-in-hand with smartphone growth, as the data center and the network become the workhorse for the smartphone.

The energy required to transfer data can vary substantially. The more the data travels over wires, the less energy is required. Wi-Fi is reasonably energy efficient. However, if data is transferred over a cellular network, energy use soars. Wireless traffic through 3G uses 15 times more energy than Wi-Fi, while 4G consumes 23 times more.

And then there's 5G, which is so fast, "you could download the entire discography of Friends AND ceremoniously drag-and-drop it in your trash bin in around the same time it would normally take to load a webpage today," web designer Scott Jehl explains. Which nicely summarizes what cheap speed does to us. When you can download anything you might possibly want in an instant, why not download everything? When the big, fat bandwidth pipe gets even bigger, we can waste to our heart's content. There'll be lots of hidden energy costs, of course. It's estimated that 5G could increase total network energy consumption by more than 150%.

At the heart of digital is a culture and mindset of waste. We have been trained not to care, to go with the flow, not to question the convenience. We must think more about energy conservation. We can't save the world if we don't conserve its energy. Always ensure you're using the most energy-efficient connection possible. Go to the extra bit of effort to regularly check your phone settings. You might end up saving yourself some money and you'll definitely be saving the Earth some energy.

60 elements

A typical smartphone will contain up to 60 materials and elements, including tin, iron, plastic, lithium, silicon, copper, nickel, alumina, silica, potassium, graphite, manganese, aluminum, tantalum, gold, silver, lead, magnesium, bromine. Producing these materials results in lots of solid and liquid waste. This waste builds up onsite in enormous dumps, sometimes several square kilometers in area. Often, these materials are mined in countries that have poor or nonexistent safety standards.

The Brumadinho dam disaster occurred in 2019 in Minas Gerais, Brazil. As the dam collapsed, the poor miners were having their meager lunch in the canteen. 250 of them were suffocated and smashed to smithereens by a tsunami-like poisonous mudflow. It seems that at the end of the logistics chain of so many of our "modern" luxuries lies a world of poor people toiling to survive. Brumadinho was by no means the first such waste dam accident and it won't be the last. "In Brazil and Minas, it is the ore above everything and everyone," explained Andréa Zhouri, of the Federal University of Minas Gerais.

Gold is used in smartphones primarily to make connectors and wires, and tin is used in the construction of the screens and in the soldering of electronics. Mining gold is a hugely wasteful process. (But not quite as wasteful as mining Bitcoin, as we'll see later.) To get enough gold for a typical ring you need to mine about 20 tons of rock and soil. Sulfuric acid, mercury and cyanide are part of the toxic sludge gold mining creates. Elemental mercury is roused by the mining process and rises, polluting the air. From Peru to Indonesia, from the Amazon to Ghana, gold mining leaves its ugly mark. Monazite, pyrochlore and xenotime are typical by-products of tin mining. They are radioactive. Tin mining is destroying rainforests and coral reefs. Planting more trees is great but we can also save the rainforests by holding on to our digital products as long as possible. Save the rainforests. Don't upgrade.

Out of the 17 rare earth metals, 16 can be found in one smartphone or another. Your phone would not be able to vibrate without neodymium and dysprosium, while terbium and dysprosium help produce those vibrant colors on the screen. Sometimes referred to as "technology metals," they are usually found in very small concentrations in the Earth. To produce one ton of a rare earth metal will typically create 2,000 tons of waste. These metals are also often found alongside radioactive materials, and the process of mining them requires carcinogenic toxins such as sulfates, ammonia and hydrochloric acid.

Who mines all this stuff that goes into our phones? Do they get treated the same way as the phone designers in California or Seoul? Do they have beanbags and ping pong tables and free lunches and ironic art on the walls of their canteens? No. At best they get minimum wages for long, arduous hours doing work that is hazardous and often life threatening. Child and slave labor are not unknown and some of the mining happens in conflict zones.

In 2019, Apple, Google, Microsoft, Dell, and Tesla were sued over their alleged reliance on cobalt mined by children. (Cobalt is a key raw material in making lithium batteries.) The poor are hidden away by the marketing slogans and cool branding. They do the dirty and dangerous work of the digital economy, so that we can throw away that two-year-old still-working phone and get the latest, must-have new one.

It doesn't have to be that way. We do have a choice. We can hang on to our phones for much longer. We can demand that the phone manufacturers make phones that can be easily repaired and recycled. We can demand that their constant software updates do not degrade the phone. We can stand up for those at the bottom of the digital logistics food chain who currently have no voice and no choice. It's not an impossible dream that all the workers that make our digital technology should be treated fairly.

In the meantime, there's lots of little practical things we can do to reduce waste. Basically, the less activity that's happening on our phones the better. Minimize notifications, disable location services, and even use airplane mode for a period every day if possible. Remove unused apps. Think long and hard before downloading a new app. Keep battery levels above 50%; short charges tend to be better for the life of your battery than long ones. Dim the screen as much as possible. Use dark mode (it can save up to 30% in battery life).

Two billion computers

"In 2019, there were over 2 billion computers in the world, including servers, desktops, and laptops," according to Supply Chain Management Outsource. A desktop uses about four to six times more power when being used than a laptop. The reason is that laptops need to operate on battery power and thus have to be more efficiently designed. Pollution flourishes where there are no constraints. The desktop is not constrained by a battery and thus the designers feel they don't need to think so much about energy efficiency.

In sleep mode, a computer or laptop is typically using about 10% of the energy it requires when it is up-and-running. Technology writer Whitson Gordon calculated that with his computer on eight hours every weekday, it was costing him about $160 per year. PC Gamer magazine estimated that running a gaming machine for two hours a day can cost from $29 to $77 a year, depending on the spec.

In the US, keeping computers running "takes the equivalent of 30 large power plants while emitting 65 million metric tons of carbon dioxide pollution," according to Pierre Delforge, writing for the Natural Resources Defense Council in 2016. We'd need to plant 6.5 billion trees to deal with that sort of pollution.

It is estimated that a typical computer spends anywhere from 50% to 77% of its time idle, doing nothing useful, creating pollution. If 30% of the time computers were turned off instead of being let sit idle, US consumers could save $3 billion a year. Delforge estimated that this would save 20 million metric tons of pollution. Instead of having to plant two billion trees to compensate for this pollution, if we turned our computers off when we're not using them, that would make a huge difference. It would have zero impact on computer performance because… we're not using them.

Here's some things to do:

- Buy a laptop instead of a desktop and get the one with the best energy ratings.
- Don't buy large screens.
- Close everything you're not actively using. Close unused windows, browser tabs and programs.

- Do not use screen savers.
- Adjust settings so that your monitor goes off after five minutes of not being used and the computer goes to sleep after 15 minutes of not being used.
- Turn your computer off at night or whenever you will not be using it for more than one hour.

Smartphone and computer addiction

Keep a watch for signs of addiction to your smartphone or computer. From the ground up, services like Facebook are designed to entrap and ensnare, to suck up as much of your attention as possible and then sell it on to advertisers. "These interfaces are intentionally designed to manipulate users," Georgetown Law School associate dean Paul Ohm stated in 2019.

In intimate detail, they know your behavioral and cognitive biases. It takes a truly conscious mind to firstly be aware that in digital you are often surrounded by dark patterns and deceptive design, and then to resist and develop immunity to these subtle and not-so-subtle nudges. It is absolutely possible to get control of your digital life. It takes time and effort, which you have more of than you might imagine. On your digital journey, think and behave like you are walking through streets full of pickpockets.

Do you get agitated when your phone isn't around or when the network is down? When you're talking to someone do you feel the compulsion to check your phone? Do you more easily get bored with face-to-face interactions and physical activities? Are you on your phone or computer when you should be sleeping? Are you constantly checking your phone or computer even when you know there's no real point? Do you pick up your phone for some reason then find yourself pointlessly browsing?

Do you turn to digital when you feel anxious or alone? Are you constantly texting while walking? When you see others using their phones do you have the compulsion to take out your phone to show that you're a busy, connected person too? Can you not go to the bathroom without using your phone? Do you find yourself on your phone or computer so as to avoid doing other stuff you know you need to do? When you know it would be much better to talk to someone or meet them face-to-face, do you still text or email?

To get a better balance in life, start by finding out how much time you're currently spending on your phone or computer. Set goals and targets. Rewards and punishments. But here's the thing. Don't set unattainable goals. Many of us set ourselves goals that we are not able to achieve, certainly not immediately. It seems that we are subconsciously setting ourselves up to fail. Set targets that are easy to achieve and then slowly expand these. Try to have a clear purpose before you pick up your phone or use your computer, and only use them for that purpose. Have places where you won't use the phone, such as at the dinner table. Do some phone fasting. You can do it. It's good for you.

Until quite recently, human societies had lots of hungry times, of forced fasting, of famines. The ability to fast became part of our DNA. Our bodies learned to use fasting in a beneficial way. Throughout history, in multiple cultures and religions, fasting has been recognized as a way to clean the body and the mind, to make us sharper and more focused. In the fifth century BC, the Greek physician Hippocrates recommended fasting to patients, and to this day fasting is recommended before many medical procedures. Fasting is a core part of Buddhism, Christianity, Hinduism, Islam, Judaism. Try some fasting from digital. It'll be good for you and chances are, after the withdrawal symptoms, you'll feel sharper and happier.

We must master digital or it will master us. We must shape digital or it will shape us. We must control digital or it will control us.

Key actions

Hold onto your digital device for as long as possible. Don't upgrade. Shut stuff off. Fast.

Links

The Global Impact of 10 Years of Smartphones, Greenpeace, 2017
http://www.greenpeace.org/usa/wp-content/uploads/2017/03/FINAL-
10YearsSmartphones-Report-Design-230217-Digital.pdf

Do you really need a new smartphone - or do you just want one? Brigitte
Osterath, DW, 2016
https://www.dw.com/en/do-you-really-need-a-new-smartphone-or-do-you-
just-want-one/a-19231144

Smartphones - not so smart for the planet, Irene Banos Ruiz, DW, 2017
https://www.dw.com/en/smartphones-not-so-smart-for-the-planet/a-
37824142

Amnesty International reports on child labor behind smartphone batteries,
Cherie Chan, DW, 2016
https://www.dw.com/en/amnesty-international-reports-on-child-labor-
behind-smartphone-batteries/a-18987204

5G Will Definitely Make the Web Slower, Maybe, Scott Jehl, Filament
Group, 2019
https://www.filamentgroup.com/lab/5g/

First Lawsuit of Its Kind Accuses Big Tech of Profiting From Child Labor
in Cobalt Mines, Edward Ongweso Jr, VICE, 2019
https://www.vice.com/en_us/article/bvg8n8/first-lawsuit-of-its-kind-
accuses-big-tech-of-profiting-from-child-labor-in-cobalt-mines

Smartphones Are Killing The Planet Faster Than Anyone Expected, Mark
Wilson, Fast Company, 2018
https://www.fastcompany.com/90165365/smartphones-are-wrecking-the-
planet-faster-than-anyone-expected

Assessing ICT global emissions footprint: Trends to 2040 &
recommendations, Lotfi Belkhir, Ahmed Elmeligi, Science Direct, 2018
https://www.sciencedirect.com/science/article/pii/S095965261733233X?via
%3Dihub

What's the environmental cost of cell phone manufacturing, really? Kayla
Matthews, Born2Invest, 2018
https://born2invest.com/articles/environmental-cost-cell-phone-
manufacturing/

Learn how to boost your smartphone battery life with these tips, Jackie
Dove, Digital Trends, 2019
https://www.digitaltrends.com/mobile/how-to-save-battery-life-on-your-
smartphone/

Our smartphone addiction is killing us – can apps that limit screen time offer a lifeline? Ashley Whillans, The Conversation, 2019
https://theconversation.com/our-smartphone-addiction-is-killing-us-can-apps-that-limit-screen-time-offer-a-lifeline-116220

12 Steps to Breaking Smartphone Addiction, Michael Pietrzak, Success, 2019
https://www.success.com/12-steps-to-breaking-smartphone-addiction/

Three ways making a smartphone can harm the environment, Patrick Byrne, Karen Hudson-Edwards, PHYS.org, 2018
https://phys.org/news/2018-08-ways-smartphone-environment.html

Facebook undermines the social belonging of first year students, Ashley V. Whillans, Frances S.Chen, Science Direct, 2018
https://www.sciencedirect.com/science/article/abs/pii/S0191886917302131?via%3Dihub

How Web Content Can Affect Power Usage, Benjamin Poulain, Simon Fraser, WebKit, 2019
https://webkit.org/blog/8970/how-web-content-can-affect-power-usage/

What to Do When Your Phone Is Eroding Your Mental Health, Jesse Hicks, VICE, 2019
https://www.vice.com/en_us/article/d3a4bz/can-being-on-your-phone-cause-depression?utm_source=vicetwitterus

Enough pixels already! TVs, tablets, phones surpass limits of human vision, experts say, Devin Coldewey, NBC News, 2013
https://www.nbcnews.com/technology/enough-pixels-already-tvs-tablets-phones-surpass-limits-human-vision-2d11691618

These are the deceptive design tricks and dark patterns that steer your clicks each day, Mark Sullivan, Fast Company, 2019
https://www.fastcompany.com/90369183/deceptive-design-tricks-and-dark-patterns-that-steer-your-clicks

How much power does my PC use? Ryan Fisher, PC Gamer, 2018
https://www.pcgamer.com/how-much-power-does-my-pc-use/

How Much Electricity Does Your PC Consume? Whitson Gordon, PC Magazine, 2019
https://uk.pcmag.com/gallery/119558/how-much-electricity-does-your-pc-consume

How many computers are there in the world? SCMO, 2019
https://www.scmo.net/faq/2019/8/9/how-many-compaters-is-there-in-the-world

How much power does a computer use? And how much CO2 does that represent? Energuide.be
https://www.energuide.be/en/questions-answers/how-much-power-does-a-computer-use-and-how-much-co2-does-that-represent/54/

Computer Energy Use Can Easily Be Cut in Half, Pierre Delforge, NRDC, 2016
https://www.nrdc.org/experts/pierre-delforge/new-report-computer-energy-use-can-easily-be-cut-half

Brazil's deadly dam disaster may have been preventable, Gabriel de Sá, National Geographic, 2019
https://www.nationalgeographic.com/environment/2019/01/brazil-brumadinho-mine-tailings-dam-disaster-could-have-been-avoided-say-environmentalists/

The Environmental Disaster That is the Gold Industry, Alastair Bland, Smithsonian Magazine, 2014
https://www.smithsonianmag.com/science-nature/environmental-disaster-gold-industry-180949762/#ISC6JfxIY5SGpeWR.99

The environmental implications of the exploration and exploitation of solid minerals in Nigeria with a special focus on Tin in Jos and Coal in Enugu, Adeyinka O. Omotehinsea, Bankole D. Akob, Science Direct, 2019
https://www.sciencedirect.com/science/article/pii/S2300396018301113

Rare Earth mining in China: the bleak social and environmental costs, Jonathan Kaiman, The Guardian, 2014
https://www.theguardian.com/sustainable-business/rare-earth-mining-china-social-environmental-costs

Understanding Food Loss and Waste—Why Are We Losing and Wasting Food? R Ishangulyyev, S Kim, S Hyeon Lee, NCBI, 2019
https://www.ncbi.nlm.nih.gov/pmc/articles/PMC6723314/

Webwaste

The Web is obese

In 1994, there were 3,000 websites. In 2019, there were estimated to be 1.7 billion, almost one website for every three people on the planet. Not only has the number of websites exploded, the weight of each page has also skyrocketed. Between 2003 and 2019, the average webpage weight grew from about 100 KB to about 4 MB. The results?

"In our analysis of 5.2 million pages," Brian Dean reported for Backlinko in October 2019, "the average time it takes to fully load a webpage is 10.3 seconds on desktop and 27.3 seconds on mobile." In 2013, Radware calculated that the average load time for a webpage on mobile was 4.3 seconds.

Study after study shows that people absolutely hate slow webpages. In 2018, Google research found that 53% of mobile site visitors left a page that took longer than three seconds to load. A 2015 study by Radware found that "a site that loads in 3 seconds experiences 22% fewer page views, a 50% higher bounce rate, and a 22% fewer conversions than a site that loads in 1 second, while a site that loads in 5 seconds experiences 35% fewer page views, a 105% higher bounce rate, and 38% fewer conversions."

The causes of webpage bloat? Images and videos are mainly to blame. By 2022, it's estimated that online videos will make up more than 82% of all consumer Internet traffic—15 times more than in 2017. However, as we'll see throughout this chapter, from the code to the content, everything about Web design has become super-bloated and super-polluting. Consider that if a typical webpage that weighs 4 MB is downloaded 600,000 times, one tree will need to be planted in order to deal with the resulting pollution.

They say a picture paints a thousand words. Well, 1,000 words of text takes up roughly two A4 (210 mm wide and 297 mm long) pages and weighs about 6 KB. You'd place about four images that are 9 cm x 16 cm on two A4 pages. Let's say these images are well optimized and weigh 40 KB each. (A poorly optimized image could weigh several megabytes.) Even with such high optimization, two A4 pages of images will weigh around 160 KB. That's 27 times more than the two A4 pages of text. A 30-second video, on the other hand, could easily weigh 3 MB. Videos create massively more pollution than text. Text is the ultimate compression technique. It is by far the most environmentally friendly way to communicate. If you want to save the planet, use more text. Think about digital weight.

From an energy point of view, it's not simply about page weight. Some pages may have very heavy processing demands once they are downloaded. Other pages, particularly those that are ad-driven, will download with lots of third-party websites hanging off them, either feeding them content, or else demanding to be fed data, often personal data on the site's visitor. It's like a type of Trojan Horse. You think you're accessing one website or app, but then all these other third parties start accessing you. According to Trent Walton, the top 50 most visited websites had an average of 22 third-party websites hanging off them. The New York Times had 64, while Washington Post had 63. All these third-party websites create pollution and invade privacy.

There is a tremendous amount of out-of-date content on websites. I have worked with hundreds of websites where we had to delete up to 90% of the pages in order to start seeing improvements. Poorly written, out-of-date code is also a major problem. By cleaning up its JavaScript code, Wikipedia estimated that they saved 4.3 terabytes a day of data bandwidth for their visitors. By saving those terabytes, we saved having to plant almost 700 trees to deal with the yearly pollution that would have been caused.

If you want to help save the planet, reduce digital weight. Clean up your website. Before you add an image, make sure that it does something useful and it's the most optimized image possible. Every time you add code, make sure it does something useful and it's the leanest code possible. Always be on the lookout for waste images, waste code, waste content. Get into the habit of removing something every time you add something.

Publishing is an addiction. Giving a website to an organization is like giving a pub to an alcoholic. You remember the saying, "There's a book inside everyone"? Well, the Web let the book out. It's happy days for a while as we all publish, publish, publish. Then…

"Hi, I'm Gerry. I have a 5,000-page website."

"Hi, Gerry."

"I used to have a 500-page website, but I had no self-control. It was one more page, one more page… What harm could one more page do?"

Redesign is rehab for websites. Every two to three years some manager either gets bored with the design or some other manager meets a customer who tells them about how horrible it is to find anything on the website. The design team rounds up a new bunch of fake images and fake content for the top-level pages, while carefully avoiding going near the heaving mess at the lower levels. After the launch, everyone is happy for a while (except the customers, of course) because in many organizations what is important is to be seen to be doing things and producing and launching things, rather than to do something useful.

If you must do something, do something useful. That often means not doing, removing, minimizing, cleaning up.

Beware the tiny tasks. We've used the Top Tasks method to identify what matters and what doesn't matter to people, whether they're buying a car, choosing a university, looking after their health, buying some sort of technology product, or whatever. In any environment we've carried it out in—and we've done it more than 500 times—there are no more than 100 things that could potentially matter.

In a health environment, these might include symptoms, treatment, prevention, costs, waiting times, etc. When buying a car they might include price, engine type, warranties, service costs, etc. We've carried out Top Tasks surveys in some 40 countries and 30 languages, with upwards of 400,000 people voting. In every single survey the same patterns emerge. Let's say there are 100 potential tasks. People are asked to vote on the tasks that are most important to them. When the results come in, we will find that five of the tasks will get the first 25% of the vote. 50 tasks will get the final 25% of the vote. The top five tasks get as much of the vote as the bottom 50. It's the same pattern in Norway, New Zealand, Israel, USA, Canada, UK, Brazil, wherever.

The bottom 50 are what I call the tiny tasks. When a tiny task goes to sleep at night it dreams of being a top task. These tiny tasks—the true waste generators—are highly ambitious and enthusiastic. They will do everything they can to draw attention to themselves, and one of the best ways of doing that is to produce lots of content, design, code.

Once we get the Top Tasks results, we sometimes analyze how much organizational effort is going into each task. Invariably, there is an inverse relationship between the importance of the task to the customer and the effort that the organization is making in relation to these tasks. The more important it is to the customer, the less is being done; the less important it is to the customer, the more is being done.

Beware of focusing too much energy, time and resources on the tiny tasks. Reducing the tiny tasks is the number one way you can reduce the number of pages and features. Save the planet. Delete the tiny tasks.

Images

I was giving a talk at an international government digital conference once, and I asked people to send me examples of where digital government was working well. One suggestion was for a website in a language I don't speak. When I visited it, I saw one of those typical big images that you see on so many websites. I thought to myself: I'm going to try and understand this website based on its images.

The big image was of a well-dressed, middle-aged woman walking down the street while talking on her phone. I put on my Sherlock Holmes hat. Hmm... Something to do with telecommunications, perhaps? Why would they choose a woman instead of a man, or a group of women and men? She's married, I deduced by looking at the ring on her finger. What is that telling me? And what about her age? Why isn't she younger or older? And why is she alone? Questions, questions, but I'm no Sherlock Holmes. I couldn't figure out anything useful from this image.

I scrolled down the page. Ah, three more images. The first one is a cartoon-like image of a family on vacation. Hmm... The next one is of two men and one woman in a room. One of them has reached their hand out and placed it on something, but I can't see what that something is, because the other two have placed their hands on top of that hand. It's a type of pledge or something, a secret society, perhaps? Two of them are smiling and the third is trying to smile. What could that mean? And then the final picture is of a middle-aged man staring into the camera, neither smiling nor unsmiling, with a somewhat kind, thoughtful look. What is happening?

I must admit that after examining all the visual evidence I had absolutely no clue what this government website was about. So, I translated it. It was about the employment conditions and legal status of government employees. Now, why didn't I deduce that from the images?

The Web is smothering us in useless images that create lots of pollution. These clichéd, stock images communicate absolutely nothing of value, interest or use. They are one of the worst forms of digital pollution and waste, as they cause page bloat, making it slower for pages to download, while pumping out wholly unnecessary pollution. They take up space on the page, forcing more useful content out of sight, making people scroll for no good reason.

Some time ago, I was looking for a pension consultant in Ireland. As I visited website after website, I noticed a pattern: a significant percentage of them were using images of the Samuel Beckett Bridge in Dublin's docklands. This is indeed a beautiful bridge. However, none of the offices of the organizations that I was looking at were located beside the bridge, and in fact one of them was located 30 kilometers away. Why do organizations so consistently use fake images and content? Why do they feel they must lie to their customers?

Lying does make sense if you're selling a product like Coke. Fakery is absolutely essential for Coke because the more you learn about the actual ingredients of Coke and the more you understand how drinking Coke damages your health, the less likely you are to buy Coke. So, it is totally essential for Coke advertising not to draw attention to the product itself but rather wrap it up in cool fakery.

However, if you're looking for a pension consultant and they all have the same fake images and the same fake content, and you can't find out about performance and fees and other important stuff, what impression do you get? Not a good one. Fake, wasteful content very often gets in the way. For every person who is fooled, there may be many more who are lost, who immediately leave the website thinking, "Never going to do business with this crowd of fakers."

Interpublic is a very large global advertising agency. As with all advertising agencies they stress how "creative" they are, which means they love huge, meaningless, happy-clappy polluting images. When I tested their homepage, it emitted almost 8 grams of CO_2 as it downloaded, putting Interpublic in the worst 10% of website polluters, according to the Website Carbon Calculator. (For comparison, the Google homepage emits 0.23 grams.) One single image on its homepage weighed 3.2 MB. This image could easily have been 10 times smaller, while losing nothing in visual appeal. The Interpublic website is like a filthy, rusty 25-year-old diesel truck, belching fumes as it trundles down the Web.

Instead of optimizing images so that they'll download faster, the opposite is often happening. TV manufacturers are now producing screens that have higher resolutions than the eye can process simply to sell gullible consumers more things they don't need. (It's essentially impossible for the eye to see the difference in the resolution of a 4K TV, for example.) It seems we can't resist "more resolution" even though we will never actually see the "more."

High-resolution images are a major cost to the environment. If, for example, you move from a 4K resolution image to an 8K one, the file size doesn't double, it trebles. For example, I saved an image at 4K and it was 6.9 MB. At 8K it was 18 MB.

Digital "progress" and "innovation" often means an increasing stress on the environment. Everything is more. Everything is higher. Everything is faster. And everything is exponentially more demanding of the environment. Digital is greedy for energy and the more it grows the greedier it gets. We need digital innovation that reduces environmental stress, that reduces the digital footprint. We need digital designers who think about the weight of every design decision they make.

We must start by trying to use the option that damages the environment least, and that is text. Don't assume that images are automatically more powerful than text. Sometimes, text does the job better.

- In a test with an insurance company, it was found that a promotion for a retirement product was deemed less accurate when an image of a face was used than when text only was used.
- Another insurance company tested a number of treatments for a promotion. The text-only treatment outperformed the image-based ones four to one.

- Yet another insurance company tried two treatments of a page for getting a quote, one with an image, one without. The page without the image had a 166% higher conversion rate.
- An initiative by the UK government to get people to sign up to become potential organ donors tested eight approaches. The approaches that used images were least effective. Text-only worked best.

"Hello?"

"Hello. Is that the Department of Useless Images?"

"Yes."

"We have this contact form and we need a useless image for it."

"How about a family cavorting in a field of spring flowers with butterflies dancing in the background?"

"Perfect."

There are indeed many situations where images are genuinely useful, particularly when it comes to helping people better understand how a product works or looks. Airbnb, for example, found that its growth only began to accelerate after it invested in getting quality images of the rental properties on offer.

If you need to use images, optimize them and consider using real ones of real people doing real things.

- A study by Marketing Experiments, in which a real photo of their client ran against one of their top-performing stock photos, found that there was a 35% higher conversion rate for the page with the real photo of the real person.
- A hair salon tested professionally-shot images of actors getting their hair done. It also shot basic images using a smartphone of ordinary clients getting their hair done. The images of ordinary clients vastly outperformed the professional images.
- A transport company used stock images and pictures of real drivers. The page with real drivers had a 38% improved conversion rate.

They say a picture paints a thousand words but sometimes it's a thousand words of crap.

Video

Video growth is exploding. Cisco estimated that by 2019 almost 80% of Internet traffic was video.

Every time you see a video, imagine you see a little diesel truck belching fumes as it trundles across the Web, because that's the impact videos have on the environment. A 30-second video can easily weigh 3 MB, so one second of video costs 300 KB. 1,000 words of text is about 6 KB. Therefore, one second of video has as much impact on the environment as 50,000 words of text, which is enough text for a pretty hefty book. Ten hours of high-definition film consumes more energy than all the English-language articles in Wikipedia put together, according to The Shift Project.

The music video for "Despacito" set an Internet record in April 2018 when it became the first video to hit five billion views on YouTube. Scientist Rabih Bashroush calculated that "Despacito" consumed as much electricity as Chad, Guinea-Bissau, Somalia, Sierra Leone and the Central African Republic would use in a year.

WPP is one of the largest advertising agencies in the world. It describes itself as "a creative transformation company." When we analyzed the website for WPP over various periods of time using Website Carbon Calculator, we found that it was consistently in the 10% of worst offenders for pollution. On the four occasions we measured it, it was emitting 5 g, 8 g, 19 g and 26 g of CO_2 when we downloaded its homepage. On one occasion, just the video that was playing weighed 5.9 MB. On the Web, WPP is like one of those filthy container ships spewing out massive toxins as it churns through the cheapest low-grade diesel.

By comparison, Google emitted 0.23 and 0.27 grams and GOV.UK emitted 0.06 g and 0.19 g when we tested them. GOV.UK estimates that it produces around 4,000 tons of CO_2 per year. We'd need to plant a little over 400,000 trees to deal with that sort of pollution, which is relatively little when you consider the number of services GOV.UK offers. Let's say we take an average pollution figure for WPP of 15 g. Using this average, WPP is emitting 115 times more pollution than GOV.UK. If WPP was running GOV.UK using its "creative" strategies, we'd need to plant almost 47 million trees to deal with its creativity.

Don't automatically assume that video is the best option. Over the years, we have watched hundreds of software engineers use technology websites to complete a wide range of tasks. Very rarely have they chosen video as their preferred option to solve a task, even when videos that would have helped them with the task were prominently displayed. They preferred text. When we explored why we discovered that text gave them more control and was faster. They could search and scroll more easily. They could get to specific pieces of information more quickly. Start with text, which is the most environmentally friendly option. Only use video when you know it makes a real difference.

Music

Like so much else, music has become so cheap it feels like it's free, and this, as we know, is the road to more frivolous consumption habits. In 1977, a vinyl record cost $28 in 2019 money. In 2019, the equivalent digital download cost $11. And of course, so much music is "free" if you're willing to pay by accepting pollution-generating, privacy-invading ads.

Digital music is good for the environment, right? No more plastic, no more vinyl, no more packaging. In 1977, the music industry used 58 million kg of plastic in the US. By 2016, as a result of digital downloading and streaming, plastic consumption had dropped to eight million kg.

However, a study by the University of Glasgow and the University of Oslo found that when the production of plastics and the generation of electricity were translated into greenhouse gas equivalents (GHGs), streaming generated very considerable amounts, which is not surprising when you consider that 3 MB would be typical for the file size of an average three-minute song.

"While GHGs peaked at 157 million in 2000 under the physical era, the generation of GHGs by storing and streaming digital files is estimated to be between 200 million kilograms and over 350 million kilograms in the USA alone," Scott Wilson wrote for FACT magazine.

The more you listen to a particular song, the more damaging it is to stream it. Therefore, for the songs you love, it's more environmentally friendly to have them on your local drive. The further what you consume has to travel, whether that is physically or digitally, the more energy is used, and the more waste is created. The closer something is to you, the less energy is consumed and the less waste is created. If you truly love it, download it. Pay for it.

JavaScript

Energy is not simply consumed as a result of the weight of a page or file being transferred or stored. Once a page is downloaded to a smartphone or computer, there is processing to do before the page becomes usable. The computer programming language called JavaScript is used for much of this processing.

Between 2011 and 2019, JavaScript file size grew by over 600%, from an average of 52 KB to 370 KB.

1 KB of JavaScript creates far more pollution than 1 KB of text, because the JavaScript is setting in train a range of energy-intensive processes. Generally, JavaScript is compressed when it is transferred. (Once it arrives in the smartphone or computer, and it is uncompressed, that 370 KB can easily become more than 1 MB.) For the average smartphone used in 2019, processing 370 KB of JavaScript could take up to 12 seconds. For older, slower phones, heavy JavaScript loads are either excruciatingly slow or else they freeze the phone entirely.

In digital, 12 seconds is an eternity. Think about it. A page with 370 KB JavaScript code may download in a flash but may not be usable for 12 seconds for millions of ordinary working people who make basic wages and have ordinary phones. Typical people, you know, trying to live a life and get by.

Some designers and developers think that the bandwidth issue is a poor country issue and not something they really need to be concerned about. "Fifteen million Americans don't have access to broadband internet," The Register reported in 2019. "For those that do, the United States has close to the slowest speeds among advanced economies. And for that, Americans pay more than almost anyone else."

Even if bandwidth increases, JavaScript-heavy pages will severely stress older or less powerful phones. It's like your phone gets hooked up to a fire hydrant whose pipes and force have been supercharged for 4G or 5G. You get flooded with stuff but that doesn't mean it's usable quickly.

Unfortunately, I have found that many digital designers and developers ignore ordinary people living on ordinary wages. Not because designers and developers are bad people. No. It's because most digital professionals live in a high-tech, large-screen, high-resolution, unlimited, high-speed bandwidth bubble. Get some fresh air out in the real world. Get out of the bubble.

On many web pages, time spent executing JavaScript far exceeds the time spent by the browser in the rest of the loading process, so minimizing JavaScript size should be a major priority.

CSS and HTML

CSS and HTML control the layout and presentation of content on a webpage. HTML is the original language of the Web that was used to lay out pages. It can easily become bloated and needs to be carefully maintained and minimized. In using CSS, it has become convenient to apply what are called "frameworks." These are all-in-one packages that contain all the CSS you might need to use and much, much more.

These frameworks might load about 100 KB of CSS. In the grand scheme of things, that's not much. However, when it comes to the Web, not every KB has the same impact. CSS must be downloaded first. Without it, the page can't be displayed. CSS thus has a critical impact on what people see and how quickly they see it. It's probable that most sites don't need any more than 10 KB of the 100 KB downloaded. Again, 90% waste.

We keep lots of CSS for the same reason that we keep lots of content and all sorts of other stuff. We don't know when in the future we might need it, or we don't know what exactly it does. We have a double whammy here. We keep it because we want to future-proof ourselves. We keep it because we're afraid to delete it. And what harm could it be doing?

The challenge of simplifying and removing the unnecessary CSS is highly complex. There are no easy-fix tools out there. "Since this problem is so hard, I think hard work is the answer to it," Web developer Chris Coyier explains. "It's understanding the problem and working toward a solution over time. A front-end developer that is intimately involved in your front end will have an understanding about what is used and unused in CSS-land after time and can whittle it down."

It's that old hard work versus convenience problem. It's about taking on some extra complexity, spending present time in order to save future time, save energy and save the environment.

Fonts

Fonts take up about 3% of data transferred while downloading an average webpage, so they are not a major contributor to energy consumption. Web browsers come with a range of standard fonts, but custom fonts allow you to choose exactly what font you want to use.

The problem is that anyone using your website has to load that font, taking up time and creating pollution. Like so much else, custom font use has exploded in recent years, growing by around 850% between 2011 and 2018. Choose a standard font unless you have a compelling reason to use a custom one.

What can you take away today?

Every image, every sentence, every line of code creates pollution because it needs energy. To **not** create today is doing something good for the environment. To reuse is better than creating. To share something lean and useful that you have created means that someone else will not now need to create that thing, thus saving energy and reducing pollution. To delete removes something that is creating pollution, because to store and transmit creates pollution.

Every day decide on at least one thing you won't do, one thing you'll reuse, one thing you'll share, one thing you'll remove.

It's not that difficult to create or to add something. To remove what needs to be removed, to see what is unnecessary, what is getting in the way, that is such an unappreciated and deep skill. Not just that, to remove requires bravery. The old logic goes: "This thing is here. It must be useful." Once things are created and published, they gain a status, an invisible protective layer. On the Web, a page can gain complexity over time because it exists within a network.

In order to remove a particular page on the Canadian Revenue Website, for example, "we had to fix over 1800ish other pages that were pointing to it," Jonathan Rath, User Experience manager, stated. "We had to go in and not just disable the link, but to re-write or remove the content on those 1800ish pages. In our world it's easy to create, hard to delete."

Weigh what you do. Wait. Is it worth it to create? Can you manage this content over its entire life? Will you be ready and willing to delete it when the time comes?

Ben Holliday, who works for the UK government, wrote about the Dutch traffic engineer Hans Monderman, who removed all traffic lights, signs, and road markings from an area in a city. That was brave. Think of all the people who would have been against that. Think of the dangers. More pedestrians might get injured, killed even. That was a potentially life-or-death decision.

"The results were the opposite of what most people expected," Ben wrote. "The traffic moved slower, people paid more attention, and accidents ultimately declined." Pay more attention to what you do. Depend less on digital and more on your own brain. You might surprise yourself by what you know. Look freshly and deeply at your digital environment. What can you take away?

Progress bar indicators are a standard element in most digital designs. It's assumed that they're a good thing, that they help people navigate through a process. Ben and his team observed that most people didn't even notice the progress bars and when they did, many got nervous or felt intimidated by them. The designers removed the progress bars. Nobody noticed that they were gone. The design was cleaner, simpler, more environmentally friendly because a team had the intelligence to ask why something was there, and the courage to remove something that didn't have a clear purpose.

What can you take away today?

Key actions

Reduce, strip away, optimize. Choose text where possible.

Every day decide on at least one thing you won't do, one thing you'll reuse, one thing you'll share, one thing you'll remove.

Links

We Analyzed 5.2 Million Desktop and Mobile Pages, Brian Dean, Backlinko, 2019
https://backlinko.com/page-speed-stats

7 Observations On The Impact Of Page Speed To The Future Of Local Mobile Search, Wesley Young, Search Engine Land, 2016
https://searchengineland.com/need-speed-7-observations-impact-page-speed-future-local-mobile-search-243128

Find out how you stack up to new industry benchmarks for mobile page speed, Daniel An, Google, 2018
https://www.thinkwithgoogle.com/marketing-resources/data-measurement/mobile-page-speed-new-industry-benchmarks/

State of the Union for Ecommerce Page Speed and Web Performance, Kent Alstad, Radware, 2015
https://blog.radware.com/applicationdelivery/wpo/2015/04/new-findings-state-union-ecommerce-page-speed-web-performance-spring-2015/

Use of images on insurance company website, F. Tranquada, T. Tullis, M. Siegel, Measuring UX, 2011
http://www.measuringux.com/presentations/LatestResearch/LatestResearch-Slides.pdf

Are people drawn to faces on webpages? T. Tullis, M. Siegel, ACM, 2009
https://dl.acm.org/citation.cfm?id=1520641

One link on GOV.UK - 350,000 more organ donors (use of images), Tom Loosemore, GOV.uk, 2014
https://gds.blog.gov.uk/2014/03/18/organ-donor-register/

Wikipedia's JavaScript initialisation on a budget, Wikipedia
https://phabricator.wikimedia.org/phame/live/7/post/175/wikipedia_s_javascript_initialisation_on_a_budget/

Mobile Videos Often Watched Without Audio, Study Finds, Jon Lafayette Broadcasting+Cable, 2019
https://www.broadcastingcable.com/news/mobile-videos-often-watched-without-audio-study-finds

Reducing page weight, DeviceAtlas, 2018
https://deviceatlas.com/blog/reducing-page-weight

US broadband is scarce, slow and expensive. 'Great!' says the FCC, Kieren McCarthy, The Register, 2018
https://www.theregister.co.uk/2018/02/06/us_broadband_fcc_report/

20 Ways to Speed Up Your Website and Improve Conversion in 2019, The Daily Egg, 2019
https://www.crazyegg.com/blog/speed-up-your-website/

Music consumption has unintended economic and environmental costs, Matt Brennan, Kyle Devine, University of Glasgow, 2019
https://www.gla.ac.uk/news/headline_643297_en.html

How streaming music could be harming the planet, Sharon George, Deirdre McKay, BBC, 2019
https://www.bbc.com/future/article/20190207-why-streaming-music-may-be-bad-for-climate-change

Climate change: Is your Netflix habit bad for the environment? BBC, 2018
https://www.bbc.com/news/technology-45798523

Measuring the climate impact of our digital services at GDS, Emily Labram, Will Pearson, GOV.uk, 2019
https://gds.blog.gov.uk/2019/10/03/measuring-the-climate-impact-of-our-digital-services-at-gds/

Do I emit CO2 when I surf the internet? Energuide.be
https://www.energuide.be/en/questions-answers/do-i-emit-co2-when-i-surf-the-internet/69/

Electricity Intensity of Internet Data Transmission, J. Aslan, K. Mayers, J. Koomey, C. France, Journal of Industrial Ecology, 2015
http://epubs.surrey.ac.uk/842520/7/Aslan_et_al-2017-Journal_of_Industrial_Ecology%281%29.pdf

Cloudwaste

Heads in the Cloud

Cloud is an abstraction and a distraction. Like so much digital, it gives the impression of lightness, impermanence, of something that is benign, of something that is good for the environment. Cloud and digital act to remove us from our physical environment and its responsibilities. We don't see the impact of our actions. We don't feel or sense that what we do in cloudland affects the land and the sea. We lead ourselves to believe that digital actions have no physical consequences.

At least our smartphones are in our hands so there is something physical there. Our computers we see and feel. If we listen carefully, we can hear the fans whir as they do their job of cooling, and sometimes we can even feel the heat these machines emit. We can turn them off if we want to. We can hold onto a USB stick or portable hard drive.

We rarely see the data centers, though, that make up the Cloud. When the Range International Information Group data center was completed in Langfang, China, in 2016, it took up 6.3 million square feet (585,000 square meters) of space, which is roughly the equivalent of 110 football fields. It's estimated that there are over eight million data centers in the world. These computing goliaths are up every minute of every hour of every day, eating electricity, sweating heat, being cooled by enormous fans, and belching pollution.

Some are proposing a more environmentally friendly approach to data center design, advising that they should be much smaller and located within cities. That would mean they would be closer to the source of data interaction, thus reducing transmission energy. It would also allow possibilities for the waste heat that is emitted by the data center to be used to heat nearby buildings. The principle is: the closer the better. The closer, the more useful waste. The greater the distance, the more useless waste. (The counter-argument is that the massive data centers run by the tech giants are much better designed and managed.)

Another principal that data center design needs to embrace is maximum utilization. 2019 analysis by 451 Research found that average server utilization rates in corporate data centers were merely 18%. In other words, 82% of the time, servers were running idle, burning electricity and pumping out pollution for zero benefit. A 2015 McKinsey analysis found even lower utilization rates: between 5% and 15%.

Amazon has claimed that server utilization rates for Cloud providers are above 50%. Like so much else in digital, the servers sit there idle, drinking electricity. If a machine is eating electricity, it should be working, not slouching around doing hardly anything, belching pollution.

Saving one gigabyte of data to the Cloud consumes approximately 0.015 kWh, while saving to your local hard disk consumes 0.000005 kWh, Justin Adamson explained in Stanford Magazine in 2017. It is therefore 3,000 times more energy intensive to save to the Cloud than to your hard disk. "When you choose to save your document to your computer, your hard drive spins up, and its mechanical arm swings across a large magnetic platter to magnetize or demagnetize the tiny cells that represent your information," Adamson wrote.

Saving a text document to the Cloud requires it to be partitioned into a stream of data packets, which then speed towards a router and then off out into the network, whizzing down lines, passing through more routers and servers, switches, repeaters, approaching the speed of light, until they enter the data center, where they will be stored and backed up, and wait until they are called again, when they will start the journey back across the airwaves, wires, routers and servers.

The greater the distance, the greater the cost to the environment. The more wireless the journey, the greater the cost to the environment. The most energy-efficient way to transfer data is through wires.

If 90% of data that is created is crap, then 90% of the activities that occur in the Cloud are waste management. There's an old saying: What do you get when you cross a fox with a chicken? You get a fox, because the fox eats the chicken. The fox is all data and the chicken is good data. All data eats the good data because the good data is much smaller than all data and all data smothers the good data. If you let all data grow, it will smother your will to do anything about it.

All data eats the planet too because there is so much of it. If immediately after you've taken those 50 photos, you delete the 45 crap ones, then you're doing something good for the environment. You're also doing something good for yourself and whoever else might get enjoyment out of those five good photos. Over time, even as you save the good ones, you will end up with 500 good ones and 50 that you really like. Take the 450 and store them locally on hard drive or USB stick.

With organizational data, it's essential to have an archive (fox), where you put the rarely-if-ever-used data that must be kept for legal reasons. This archive will use cold, deep storage systems, where data will not be so immediately accessible. Such storage systems can save up to 90% on energy costs. Put the fox into cold, deep storage.

Static can be good

Always choose the least energy-intensive option to get the job done. If less does the job, use less. A database-driven website is a bit like having a seven-seater car. If there's only two in your household, do you really need it? Perhaps a simpler, more energy-efficient static website is better? I used to make these sorts of arguments a lot about 15 years ago, and then for whatever reason I stopped making them and I started using databases for our websites because everyone else was doing it and it was more convenient.

Most websites today are database driven. This means that the content, code and other components are stored and delivered from a database. The pages on the site don't actually exist permanently. Rather, when you click on a link for a page or type the URL in, the page is dynamically created, going into the database to fetch all the relevant content, code and components. A database website is very effective when things are likely to be constantly changing, for example stock levels for a particular product.

The alternative to a database website is what is called a "static website." This is a website whose pages permanently exist. A great many websites do not need to be dynamically created from a database because they don't change much. They can work perfectly well as static sites. A static page will load faster and will require less processing, thus saving energy. That's good for the customer and it's good for the environment.

We did an experiment on my website gerrymcgovern.com, where we tested how long it took the site to load on a smartphone direct from a database and as a static website.

There are two basic ways to measure how fast a page loads. The first measure concerns how quickly some content becomes visible, preferably text, so that there's something you can read. Based on this metric, the static page loaded in 2.9 seconds and the database-driven version took 4.7 seconds to load. The second metric analyzes how quickly the page becomes usable, so how long until you can start booking your flight or whatever. Based on this metric, the static page loaded in 2.9 seconds and the database-driven version took 5 seconds to load.

What's a couple of seconds, you might ask?

1. For every second faster Walmart.com was able to make its pages load, it had a 2% lift in conversions.

2. Firefox reduced its page load time by 2.2 seconds and had 10 million extra downloads as a result.

3. Financial Times found that a one-second delay in page loads caused a 4.9% drop in the number of articles read. A three-second delay caused a 7.2% drop.

4. "A site that loads in 3 seconds experiences 22% fewer page views, a 50% higher bounce rate, and a 22% fewer conversions than a site that loads in 1 second," a study by Radware found.

5. Google discovered that even a 400-millisecond delay could result in eight million fewer searches per day. (That's less than half a second.)

6. Amazon found that a page load slowdown of only one second could cost it $1.6 billion in sales each year.

Time matters. Static websites are faster. I have seen analysis that indicates that a static website can be up to 10 times faster than an equivalent database-driven site. In our analysis, when the page was static, 378 KB of data was being transferred. When the page was served from a database, 701 KB was being transferred. That's almost twice the data transfer for a database-driven page. Imagine all the energy and time that could be saved if the millions of websites that don't need to be database driven migrated to static? We must think about the energy. We must think about the data. We must think about the pollution.

If static websites are better in many situations, why aren't they used more? Why have we in fact moved in the opposite direction? "Progress," "innovation," the desire to be seen to be using the "latest" technology. A database is more "advanced" than a static website, and everyone wants to be seen as more advanced. We are willing zombies in the march of progress, assuming that innovation and what is new are always better. We are so enamored by more power and more processing and more complexity that we believe that more always delivers better, and that we must always have more. We don't understand "enough" power, we only understand "more" power. We want the highest spec, always the highest spec.

We must become much more questioning of energy, power, innovation, new things, and the impact that all our actions—both digital and physical—have on this beautiful and stressed planet we call home. How much is needed to do the job? If we can do the job with 1X power, let's do it with 1X. Why do we need 10X when 1X will do? We can stop creating 9X pollution and still have everything we want. Use what is needed to get the job done, no more, no less.

Search

Google estimates that carrying out a single search takes about 0.0003 kWh (1080 joules) of energy. That's the equivalent of leaving a 60-watt bulb on for 17 seconds. In 1999, it was estimated that there were one billion searches on Google. In 2019, there were 5.2 billion searches a day, and 1.9 trillion searches a year. That's the equivalent of leaving a 60-watt bulb on for one million years.

1.9 trillion yearly searches consume 569,400,000 kWh of electricity. According to RenSMART this creates 161,180,000 kg of CO_2. To offset the pollution from 1.9 trillion searches would require the planting of 16 million trees.

Like so much else in digital, Google search is a new weight for the Earth to carry, one that is growing in leaps and bounds. In 1999, for example, to absorb the pollution from one billion searches, it would only have required the planting of 8,500 trees. In 20 years, the weight of search has become 1,900 times heavier for the Earth to bear.

If a single search costs 0.0003 kWh of energy, then if we translate that into calories, one search burns 0.26 calories in equivalent energy resources. If we assume that a typical search takes 10 seconds then, based on the Basal Metabolic Rate, the human body burns 0.16 calories during a search. Thus, every search costs the Earth 0.1 more in calories than it costs the searcher. If we were running at 5 mph (8 kmph) for 10 seconds, then we would burn about 1.7 calories. If we were walking at 2.5 mph (4 kmph) we would burn 0.85 calories in 10 seconds.

Much of our interaction with digital is sedentary and slow from a human-energy-consumption perspective. 80% of teenagers globally are too inactive—and it could shorten their lives, according to a 2019 WHO study. Digital makes us burn more of the Earth's resources than our own. Our own energy resources, of course, originally resided in the Earth as plants or animals. However, now they reside in us and if we don't burn them, we waste energy and we potentially damage our bodies through lack of exercise.

Some of this energy the body will try not to waste. It will turn it into fat, which is the body's battery. For many, this battery will grow in size and corrode because it will not be used. The danger of digital is that the convenience it delivers creates short-term highs with long-term costs for us and the planet.

Google claims that their data centers are highly efficient and use sustainable energy where possible. However, we know that most digital energy is used not in the processing, storage or transmission of data but in the manufacture of the machines used to do the work. It's estimated that Google uses about two million servers at any one time. These servers will have consumed most of their energy during their manufacture. They will have short, underutilized lives, and when they die, they will be dumped as toxic waste.

Twitter, Facebook

It's estimated that each tweet consumes about 90 joules of electricity, which is about one-tenth what a typical search would consume. (Although a tweet with an image would consume considerably more.) Each tweet will thus emit about 0.02 grams of CO_2.

In 2010, there were roughly 50 million tweets per day, delivering about one ton of CO_2 into the atmosphere or 365 tons per year. By 2019, there were an average of 500 million tweets per day. Thus, the annual pollution for Twitter would be in the region of 3,650 tons. We'd need to plant about 330,000 trees to offset that. Facebook created 339,000 tons of CO_2 in 2018, according to Statista. We'd need to plant 31 million trees to offset that pollution.

Key actions

Conserve the Earth's energy. Spend your own. Focus on the Earth Experience.

Only use as much digital as is needed to get the job done. Use Google less. Use your brain and memory more.

Keep your data local. Only keep the essential, current stuff in the Cloud.

Links

Energy Hogs: Can World's Huge Data Centers Be Made More Efficient? Fred Pearce, Yale Environment 360, 2018
https://e360.yale.edu/features/energy-hogs-can-huge-data-centers-be-made-more-efficient

CHC – A conceptual approach to sustainable & scalable Digital Infrastructure, SDIA, 2019
https://sdia.cdn.prismic.io/sdia%2F6c331e9b-5d57-4402-88d3-d40a06a01933_chc_conceptpaper_0108.19.pdf

Server utilization rates, Mike Wheatley, SiliconANGLE, 2019
https://siliconangle.com/2019/11/26/aws-says-businesses-move-cloud-lower-carbon-footprint/

Server utilization: 30% Of Servers Are Sitting "Comatose" According To Research, Ben Kepes, Forbes, 2015
https://www.forbes.com/sites/benkepes/2015/06/03/30-of-servers-are-sitting-comatose-according-to-research/

Powering a Google Search: The Facts and Figures, Direct Energy, 2017
https://business.directenergy.com/blog/2017/november/powering-a-google-search

Majority of adolescents worldwide are not sufficiently physically active, putting their current and future health at risk, WHO, 2019
https://www.who.int/news-room/detail/22-11-2019-new-who-led-study-says-majority-of-adolescents-worldwide-are-not-sufficiently-physically-active-putting-their-current-and-future-health-at-risk

Computer factories eat way more energy than running the devices they build, Michael Cooney, NETWORKWORLD, 2011
https://www.networkworld.com/article/2229029/computer-factories-eat-way-more-energy-than-running-the-devices-they-build.html

Designing for Sustainability: A Guide to Building Greener Digital Products and Services, Tim Frick, O'Reilly Media, 2016
http://shop.oreilly.com/product/0636920043904.do

6 Reasons Why You Should Go for a Static Website, Tanya Kumari, DZone, 2018
https://dzone.com/articles/6-reasons-why-you-should-go-for-a-static-website

Carbon and the Cloud, Justin Adamson, Stanford Magazine, 2017
https://medium.com/stanford-magazine/carbon-and-the-cloud-d6f481b79dfe

How Much Energy Per Tweet? Katie Fehrenbacher, GIGAOM, 2010
https://gigaom.com/2010/04/19/how-much-energy-per-tweet/

Greenhouse gas emissions released by Facebook from 2014 to 2018,
Statista, 2018
https://www.statista.com/statistics/580123/Facebook-carbon-footprint-and-ghg-emissions/

Ads are the oil industry of the Web

No free lunches

You're being watched. You're being tracked. You're being profiled. You're being measured. Your value is being weighed. Your every digital interaction leaves a data trail and these data trails are hoovered up by a dark web of surveillance companies. There's a lot to hoover up. Much of Big Data is personal data.

Using sources from Every Day Big Data Statistics and Cisco, in 2016 Shaun Norris calculated that the average Internet user generates about half a gigabyte of data per day. That's about 180 GB a year. According to Statista, "almost 4.48 billion people were active Internet users as of October 2019." You'd need to plant almost 340 million trees to deal with the pollution caused by the personal data we generate on the Internet. It's like when we're online we're belching CO_2.

Frederike Kaltheuner, a tech policy fellow at Mozilla, has researched how much data was being collected on her. In just one week, a dark web (but totally legal) company called Quantcast "has amassed over 5,300 rows and more than 46 columns worth of data including URLs, time stamps, IP addresses, cookies IDs, browser information and much more." Quantcast also had information on her gender, age, presence of children in her household (in number and ages), her education level, and gross yearly household income. All to target her with ads, though, as we'll see later, this sort of targeting isn't quite as effective as some dreamt it would be.

In the economy of free, the Earth pays. The economy of free is a hugely wasteful economy because it gives one million people a carrot in order to get one sucker to buy a juicer. The economy of free is a hugely wasteful economy because it is primarily an economy of wants rather than of needs. Why not download the app? It's free. You may not use it more than once, but so what? It's free.

I need a place to stay. I want to stay in a 5-star hotel at a 3-star price. The advertiser wants me to pay a 4-star price, or at least stay in their 5-star 3-star-price hotel. That requires a lot of targeting, a lot of persuasion, and all that requires a lot of energy. The energy to collect enough data on me to know that I am a good target. The energy to create highly emotional, visual advertising. The energy to track me and keep showing me this advertising wherever I go. That's a lot of pollution.

The global online advertising industry is enormous. At over $300 billion in turnover, 2019 was the first year that more was spent advertising online than offline. ($300 billion, by the way, is the amount UN scientists estimate is needed to create sustainable solutions for climate change.) eMarketer estimates that online advertising will be worth more than $500 billion by 2023. Online advertising is horrendously wasteful, but that's nothing new.

Offline advertising depends on "magic" and "creativity" and made-up numbers. Search-based advertising is much less wasteful than traditional advertising because the roles are essentially reversed. The searcher becomes the advertiser. When they search for "cheap flights Dublin," they are advertising that they want to find a cheap flight to Dublin. It is then up to companies to respond to that ad with an offer of cheap flights to Dublin. That is a much more energy-efficient form of advertising because you've got a buyer with a demand that has been made clear (cheap flights Dublin) and a seller who can meet that demand.

As a result, it is estimated that for every 100 people that see a Google search ad, three will click on it. Three out of 100. That is regarded as a mind-bogglingly good metric by advertisers. Imagine if for every 100 people who walked into a restaurant only three stayed. Wouldn't be very good, would it? But three out of 100 has made Google Google and Facebook Facebook. In the hugely wasteful world of advertising, three out of 100 is the most amazing of the most amazing success.

Now, let's give it a little twist so as to bring traditional advertising into perspective. When was the last time you searched for "cheap flights new york" and ended up buying golf clubs instead, because you saw this amazing ad for golf clubs and it made you totally forget that what you really wanted to do was buy a cheap flight to New York? Doesn't happen, does it? Happens in advertising magicland, at least that's what the magical advertisers tell us.

When it comes to the more traditional visual banner ads, it takes 2,000 people to see such ads before one will click. This data is suspect, as so much data about the Web is, because it seems that 8% of people who do click account for 85% of clicks, comScore reported. Are these people "people" or are they bots masquerading as people? Or perhaps they are people but poor people working as click slaves, clicking and clicking on ads so as to defraud advertisers?

You see, just because people click on an ad doesn't mean a lot. If you want to measure value, you must measure how many people actually bought the thing that was advertised in the ad. (And, as we'll see later, you must know whether they bought it because they saw the ad, or whether they were going to buy it anyway whether they saw the ad or not.)

A 2015 study of 58 online ad campaigns, as reported by Science Direct, found that over 50% of them saw less than one purchase per million times the ad was seen. (This was considered an excellent result by ad executives.) Think about that for a moment. The ad was "seen" 999,999 times and no purchase occurred. All that pollution. Again, the economics are all wrong. The models we have today are designed to consume the Earth's resources for short-term gain. The Earth pays for online advertising. Our children and grandchildren will pay for the wanton waste that is online advertising. If it's free, the Earth's paying.

According to Google, the maximum file size for a banner ad is 150 KB. Let's take 100 KB as an average. If a typical banner needs to be seen one million times in order to achieve a purchase, then that's 100,0000,000 KB, which is 100 GB. Transmitting one GB consumes about 0.015 kWh of electricity. For 100 GB that gives us 1.5 kWh which creates about 0.42 kg of CO_2, according to RenSMART, for each banner ad over its lifetime.

Are these figures exactly correct? Maybe not. But what we do know with absolute certainty: It's not zero. Every ad costs the planet. Every ad is based on a hugely wasteful model.

Online advertising costs you and me money as well, particularly if you are accessing the Internet with your smartphone using a data plan. For example, the cost of one GB of mobile broadband can be about $10 in the US and $7 in the UK. Prices vary a lot. The poorer you are, the more you tend to pay per GB because of the nature of the plans available. This is ironic because advertising is more and more targeted at the poor, since better-educated and better-off people have become more immune to ads. As economics professor Scott Galloway puts it, "Advertising is a tax the poor and technologically illiterate pay."

It's estimated that US citizens are exposed to thousands of ads every day, and about 55 of these are online banner ads. Thus, every day it costs a typical smartphone user in the US about six cents to download banner ads, or about $1.90 a month. It could in fact be much higher. In 2015, The New York Times, in a study of the mobile homepages of the top 50 news websites, found that more than half of all data transfers came from ads. The study estimated that for someone using a typical smartphone data plan, the ads alone on visiting Boston.com every day would cost them $9.50 a month.

What we've measured above is the cost of the file size of the ad. There are many more costs, not least the costs associated with designing and approving the ads. Apps with ads have been found to use an average of 16% more battery power, and sometimes up to 33% more, while consuming up to 50% of a phone's processing power, because of all the tracking software that hangs off them. According to a 2018 study by Solarwinds, the average load time for the top 50 websites was 9.46 seconds with ads, and 2.69 seconds without. So, a website with ads took more than three times longer to download than one without. The same study found 298 pieces of tracking and personal data collection software on the top 50 websites. 75% of these trackers were ad-related.

In summary, online advertising increases energy consumption because:
1. Much more data needs to be downloaded both for the ad itself and the huge amount of tracking software that comes with it.
2. Much more processing needs to occur.
3. The ads are constantly communicating across the network. Even when you're not viewing the page, the ads are constantly sending bursts of energy-sapping data back to their motherlode in the data center.

Malpractice

Online advertising is full of fraud and malpractice. Data has shown that if you are Ford, for example, then buying ads when people search for "Ford" is not that effective because you're going to reach those people anyway. However, if you are Ford and you buy ads to appear when someone searches for "Toyota" then that can be quite effective.

"Don't be evil" has been the Google tagline, mission statement, guiding philosophy from practically day one of its existence. In 2018, it quietly dropped the "don't" from the tagline. Google was entering a new phase of sucking up personal data and manipulating search results and spewing out giganormous profits.

Do you remember back in those innocent, hippy, don't-be-evil days, when Google placed the ads in the right-hand column so as to clearly differentiate them from the organic search results? Ah, those naïve do-gooder, don't-be-evil hippies that they were. We didn't deserve them. Thing was, very few people looked in the right-hand column and even fewer people clicked. So, poor Google was only making billions from ads instead of the gazillions they dreamt of.

They quietly moved the ads to the top of the central column. And so that everyone would know that these were ads, they placed a teeny-weensy sign saying "Ad." Such ethical dudes and dudesses. People are so stupid, though. Studies indicate that between 50% and 60% of people don't actually know that the ads are ads. Google must be so upset about that.

That was just the beginning of nefarious activities for the rebranded "Be Evil" empire. Not satisfied with greying the line between ads and organic search results, Google decided to get into the highly lucrative Mafia Don business of shaking down companies for protection money. "When Google puts 4 paid ads ahead of the first organic result for your own brand name, you're forced to pay up if you want to be found," Jason Fried, founder of Basecamp states. "It's a shakedown. It's ransom."

Like all good Mafiosi, Google targets vulnerable industry after vulnerable industry, looking for their protection money. Take travel. "TripAdvisor has one of the best link profiles of any commercially oriented website outside of perhaps Amazon.com," search optimization expert Aaron Wall writes. "But ranking #1 doesn't count for much if that #1 ranking is below the fold. Or, even worse, if Google literally hides the organic search results." The result? Google grows its ad revenues 20% a year in a global economy growing at under 4%, and the stocks of Expedia and TripAdvisor fall off cliffs. That's advertising for you.

Outright fraud

It's hard to deal with fraud when your industry is founded on it. Advertising so often depends on getting celebrities or "influencers" to peddle their wares. If brands can't afford celebrities, then at least they'll get beautiful happy people with amazing teeth to fake it.

Online, ad fraud has been taken to a new level. Why pay a celebrity to pretend they use your product when you can just steal their image. You can have them say exactly what you want for nothing. You can get them to claim that Product X has magical properties that will transform the life of all who buy it. How different is that from traditional advertising? Celebrities make wild claims all the time about products they probably don't even use. When it comes to advertising, it's hard to identify what is fraud and what is fake.

Julien has a popular app that depends on ads for revenue. "Julien sells a banner ad, which appears in the app and is visible to his users," Craig Silverman writes for BuzzFeed. "Then, hidden from view behind that banner, fraudsters conceal autoplaying video ads that no human being actually sees, but which register as having been served and viewed. In this scenario, Julien gets paid for the small banner ad in his app that users see, but the fraudsters earn many times that amount by stuffing far more lucrative video ads behind the banner." All those fraudulent video ads running in the background are pumping out loads of pollution.

It's estimated that less than 60% of web traffic is human, with a large proportion of the rest being ad fraud bots clicking, clicking, clicking on ads. At one stage there were so many bots "watching" stuff on YouTube that management feared that their algorithms would start seeing the bots as normal and the humans as abnormal. Ad fraud costs billions every year but nobody really has a clue exactly how much, because when it comes to digital metrics, you're entering a world of fakery, manipulation and magical thinking.

Facebook took down 2.2 billion fake accounts between January and March 2019, CNN reported. That's an awful lot of fake accounts. Amazingly, only in 2019 did Facebook begin a proper auditing process for its ads. In 2016, it was estimated that 85% of "people" "watching" Facebook ads were "watching" with the sound off. Big fanbase for silent movies, I suppose. What was the solution? Captions for videos! In 2019, Facebook settled a legal complaint that stated that the average viewership metrics for video ads were inflated by between 150% and 900%.

Facebook, the company that pursues growth and profit over everything, has revolutionized ad fraud with its wonderful tools that can help criminals target the needy, weak and gullible. As one fraudster put it: "They go out and find the morons for me." Advertising has a history of targeting the gullible, the weak, the poor, the uneducated, the needy. Online, it's no different.

Magical thinking

You might imagine that behind the scenes there is a big gang of evil geniuses figuring out the next way to trick and manipulate customers. You'd be wrong. Many organizations may be swimming in a sea of customer data but most of that sea is as polluted as our normal seas. "The majority of advertising companies feed their complex algorithms silos full of data even though the practice never delivers the desired result," Jesse Frederik and Maurits Martijn wrote for The Correspondent.

Back around 2000, when a senior advertising executive was shown how Google worked, he wasn't impressed. "You're fucking with the magic" was his reply. In a different period, a manager from a brand was supposed to have said, "50% of my advertising works. I don't know which 50%." Google was promising to identify which 50%, and that was deeply worrying to traditional advertising executives, as transparency was the last thing they wanted in the advertising industry.

Advertisers pride themselves on being creative—as in "creative accounting." They make shit up. Invent stuff to make their clients feel happy. They tell fabulous, magical lies to audiences that want to believe fabulous, magical lies.

For a while, Google did "fuck with the magic," at least in relation to search-based advertising, which was much more transparent than traditional advertising had ever been. However, outside the realm of search-based advertising, online has turned out to be as big a world of magical thinking for advertising as the physical world was. For all the data, the metrics are still sprinkled with the magical dust of hype and buzzwords. In fact, if anything, data is overwhelming many organizations' ability to be effective.

Although an incredible amount of personal data is collected, a great deal of it is never even used, because most organizations are not capable of managing data effectively. Instead, there is an obsession with big numbers and more volume. The volume metrics are often much more about how to make the higher-ups look good and feel good.

There is an obsession with meaningless concepts such as "engagement" and "interactivity," "innovation" and creating things that go swish and swoosh, and making senior managers feel like they're directors in a James Bond movie. Innovation is absolutely essential, whatever that means. When you boil it all down, so much of it is about the primal instinct to have more, to have a bigger whatever. It's the Cult of Volume. Welcome to the Short-Term Growth Club.

Inventing high volume, meaningless metrics "makes everyone happy," David Reiley, former head of Yahoo's economics team explained to The Correspondent. "It will make the publisher happy. It will make the person who bought the media happy. It will make the boss of the person who bought the media happy. It will make the ad agency happy. Everybody can brag that they had a very successful campaign."

Volume-based metrics have always been open to fraud and manipulation. The Irish police are responsible for saving lives on the roads by ensuring drunk drivers are found and prosecuted. That's the desired outcome, but it was not the key metric for the police. The key volume metric that met targets and ensured promotions was how many drink-driving tests had been carried out. Oh, those big numbers, how management loves those big numbers. Of course, such input-focused, volume-based metrics are so much easier to manipulate. The Irish police kept inventing and inflating the huge and humongous number of tests they were carrying out, which showed to anyone that would listen what hard-working boys and girls they were.

Unfortunately, someone finally asked the very awkward question: "If you're doing all these tests, how come you've so few convictions?" It's much harder to manipulate data on the outcome (convictions for drunk driving). Focus on measuring the outcome if you want to establish true value.

Personalization was a wonder drug, an all-conquering magical tool that would personalize everything. Collect all this rich customer data and then micro-target the hell out of people. Sounded great in theory. However, to design and maintain such personalization systems takes a tremendous effort. I have seen personalization situations that required four to five times the investment in personnel than that required for running the same non-personalized website.

These people are not cheap. You need data analysts who can keep the data clean and accurate. You need designers, developers and content professionals continuously improving the environment, because personalization is notoriously difficult to optimize for.

Personalization is really, really hard work, fraught with privacy concerns, and at the end of the day often doesn't deliver anywhere near the returns promised. Therefore, it was not surprising that in 2019 Gartner predicted that 80% of marketers would abandon their personalization efforts by 2025 "due to lack of ROI, the perils of customer data management or both." The data, the promise of all that data, it wasn't working the way the ads said it would. All that data collected for nothing. Waste. To be piled with all the other waste data in one more data dump in the Cloud.

What's the answer? What's the solution? Less data. Better quality. A much greater focus on customer outcomes, rather than organizational inputs. Much more analysis and thought.

Don't feed the ads. Don't click on the ad. Click on the natural search result instead. Because the more you click on the ads, the more they think you're one of the gullible ones, and then they will relentlessly, relentlessly target you and sell you to others to relentlessly target.

Pay for stuff. Nothing is free. When it's free, the Earth pays, you pay with bandwidth and your personal data is the product that's sold to advertisers. Try it out for free, sure, but then have a serious, intense conversation with yourself. Is this app genuinely delivering value to my life? If yes, pay for it. You're helping yourself, the environment and the app creator. You're helping create a value-based economy rather than an ad-based economy.

If you make an app, sure, offer a free version, but if you can't get people to pay, then question whether you are making something of genuine value, or are you one more waste creator, living off the advertising, living off the planet?

Just Do It. How about: Don't Do It. Wait. Don't download, don't click, don't buy. Do stuff with what you already have. Wear stuff out, use your stuff. Find ways to get what you need done with what you already have. Be inventive. Be creative. Be an innovator in your own life using the materials you already have. Weigh up everything you do. Is it worth it?

Key actions

Don't feed the ads. Don't click on the ad. Find the organic search result and click on it. Organic is better.

Find out what you truly value. Pay for it.

Links

How much digital data does an average digital user generate per day and per year? Shaun Norris, Quora, 2016
https://www.quora.com/How-much-digital-data-does-an-average-digital-user-generate-per-day-and-per-year

RenSMART carbon emissions calculator
https://www.rensmart.com/Calculators/KWH-to-CO2

Website Carbon Calculator
https://www.websitecarbon.com/

How A Massive Facebook Scam Siphoned Millions Of Dollars From Unsuspecting Boomers, Craig Silverman, BuzzFeed, 2019
https://www.buzzfeednews.com/article/craigsilverman/Facebook-subscription-trap-free-trial-scam-ads-inc

Facebook removed 2.2 billion fake accounts in three months, Kaya Yurieff, CNN, 2019
https://edition.cnn.com/2019/05/23/tech/facebook-transparency-report/index.html

How Facebook Helps Shady Advertisers Pollute the Internet, Zeke Faux, Bloomberg, 2018
https://www.bloomberg.com/news/features/2018-03-27/ad-scammers-need-suckers-and-facebook-helps-find-them

Facebook Settles Class Action Claiming Company Inflated Video Viewership Metrics, Eriq Gardner, Hollywood Reporter, 2019
https://www.hollywoodreporter.com/thr-esq/facebook-settles-class-action-claiming-company-inflated-video-viewership-metrics-1218059

Environmental impact assessment of online advertising, M. Pärssinena, M. Kotilab R. Cuevasc, A. Phansalkard, J. Mannere, Science Direct, 2018
https://www.sciencedirect.com/science/article/pii/S0195925517303505

These U.N. Climate Scientists Think They Can Halt Global Warming for $300 Billion. Here's How, Adam Majendie, Pratik Parija, TIME, 2019
https://time.com/5709100/halt-climate-change-300-billion/

How Much of the Internet Is Fake? Turns Out, a Lot of It, Actually, Max Read, New York Magazine, 2018
https://nymag.com/intelligencer/2018/12/how-much-of-the-internet-is-fake.html

The Effect of Ad Blockers on the Energy Consumption of Mobile Web Browsing, Arthur Visser, University of Twente, 2016
https://pdfs.semanticscholar.org/c2f4/b15d53eeeabbe41e918eefffa9321978f82d.pdf

After GDPR, The New York Times cut off ad exchanges in Europe — and kept growing ad revenue, Jessica Davies, DIGIDAY, 2019
https://digiday.com/media/gumgumtest-new-york-times-gdpr-cut-off-ad-exchanges-europe-ad-revenue/

The Cost of Mobile Ads on 50 News Websites, G. Aisch, W. Andrews, J. Keller, New York Times, 2015
https://www.nytimes.com/interactive/2015/10/01/business/cost-of-mobile-ads.html

Pixalate Says 30% Of Programmatic Ad Impressions In Australia Are Invalid… So Is Online Advertising A Scam? Edward Pollitt, Bandt, 2019
https://www.bandt.com.au/advertising/online-advertising-problems

Ads in free mobile apps have hidden costs for both users and developers, Robert Perkins, University of Southern California, 2015
https://www.sciencedaily.com/releases/2015/04/150401093623.htm

'A daily, hourly fight': Digital ad fraud is worse than ever, January 9, 2019, Jessica Davies, Digiday, 2019
https://digiday.com/media/daily-hourly-fight-digital-ad-fraud-worse-ever/

The new dot com bubble is here: it's called online advertising, Jesse Frederik, Maurits Martijn, The Correspondent, 2019
https://thecorrespondent.com/100/the-new-dot-com-bubble-is-here-its-called-online-advertising/13230718600-5d15791f

The good, the bad and the troubling: trust in advertising hits record low, Gideon Spanier, Campaign, 2019
https://www.campaignlive.co.uk/article/good-bad-troubling-trust-advertising-hits-record-low/1524250

The Cost Of Mobile Internet Around The World, Niall McCarthy, Forbes, 2019
https://www.forbes.com/sites/niallmccarthy/2019/03/05/the-cost-of-mobile-internet-around-the-world-infographic/

The 45 Most Important Advertising Statistics of 2019 (banner ad exposure), Milja Milenkovic, Smallbizgenius, 2019
https://www.smallbizgenius.net/by-the-numbers/advertising-statistics/

Gartner Predicts 80% of Marketers Will Abandon Personalization Efforts by 2025, Gartner, 2019
https://www.gartner.com/en/newsroom/press-releases/2019-12-02-gartner-predicts-80--of-marketers-will-abandon-person?

I asked an online tracking company for all of my data and here's what I found, Frederike Kaltheuner, Privacy International, 2018
https://privacyinternational.org/long-read/2433/i-asked-online-tracking-company-all-my-data-and-heres-what-i-found

Almost 60% of People Still Don't Recognise Google Paid Ads When They See Them, Varn, 2018
https://varn.co.uk/01/18/varn-original-research-almost-60-people-still-dont-recognise-google-paid-ads-see/

AI rising

A brief history of life

The Earth formed about 4.5 billion years ago. It is believed that life began to emerge about 800 million years later. Humans evolved from apes around three million years ago, with modern humans emerging only about 200,000 years ago.

The evolution of computers is generally described in generations. The first generation (1940–1956) used vacuum tubes and could take up the space of an entire room. The second generation (1956–1963) replaced vacuum tubes with transistors, making computers smaller and faster. The third generation (1964–1971) introduced the integrated circuit, making computers even smaller and faster. The microprocessor heralded the fourth generation of computers (1972–2010). This allowed for the development of desktops and laptops. The fifth generation (from 2010 to present) has seen the emergence of artificial intelligence (AI).

In 80 years, we moved through five generations of computing. Between 1956 and 2015 there was a one-trillion-fold increase in computing performance. The Apollo Guidance Computer that landed humans on the moon had the equivalent power of two Nintendo entertainment systems. The Apple iPhone 4, launched in 2010, had the same power as the Cray-2 supercomputer, launched in 1985.

Cuneiform is the earliest known language and emerged about 3,400 years ago in the area we now call Iraq. Cuneiform was written with a reed stylus on wet clay tablets. These tablets still exist and are perfectly readable, and as philologist Irving Leonard Finkel assures us, they will exist long after today's computer storage has vanished.

In achieving speed, power and greater capacity, computer technology has traded longevity, durability and reliability.

A typical processor or piece of storage has an extremely short life expectancy of about five years. The resource and waste implications of this are enormous. If a clay tablet had a life expectancy of five years, we would have had to replace each tablet about 680 times since the information was first written down.

"Speaker company Sonos will cut off its most loyal customers from future software updates entirely unless they replace their old equipment for newer models," The Guardian reported in 2020. These "smart" speakers and all the other smart networked stuff in the world of the Internet of Things (IoT) have very short lives. The hardware of the speaker may be working perfectly well but if the software is not updated then the product quickly degrades until it reaches a point whether it does not function and/or it becomes a security risk. This is a recipe for tremendous waste, pollution, and privacy violations.

Computer technology has had—and will continue to have—a ferocious appetite for energy and material resources. Artificial intelligence (AI) is a child that is growing at a phenomenal rate. It has taken modern humans 200,000 years and about 10,000 generations to get where we are today. In five generations, spanning 80 years, AI has emerged.

Lee Se-dol became a professional Go player at age 12. Go is a tremendously complex board game originating in China several thousand years ago. When computers finally beat humans at chess, I remember some saying that while computers might master chess, they would never master Go, a game of almost endless possibilities. Go was described as the Holy Grail of AI, with Lee Se-dol the Roger Federer of Go. In 2016, Google-owned AI program AlphaGo defeated Lee. In 2019, he retired from Go, saying simply that AI "cannot be defeated."

I've been following the evolution of Artificial Intelligence (AI) for more than 30 years. The power and potential always seemed awesome. AI is still in its infancy, though it is learning fast. At what point it develops an independent intelligence, it's hard to know, though it seems inevitable that AI will quickly evolve into something superior to human intelligence on many levels. When AI is combined with robotics, the path to artificial life is clear. Humans are as powerless to stop the evolution of AI as the apes were powerless to stop the evolution of humans.

Properly applied, AI can save energy and support the more efficient management of the environment. AI can help optimize water, energy and traffic management. AI-managed drones can plant trees 150 times faster than traditional methods. They can analyze soils and deliver targeted and precise fertilizer or weedkiller, increasing yields and reducing overall fertilizer and pesticide usage. In Brazil, honeybees are wearing Internet of Things (IoT) devices so that we can better understand the causes of colony collapse. AI has been found to be better than radiologists at diagnosing breast cancer from mammograms.

The questions are:
- Will the energy that AI saves be greater than the energy it consumes?
- Will the waste that AI helps eliminate be greater than the waste it creates?
- Will the benefits be greater than the costs?

Hungry AI

AI has developed a savage appetite for energy. Up until 2012, the amount of computing power required to train and feed an AI model roughly doubled every two years. Then it started doubling every three to four months. The energy efficiency of AI models, on the other hand, is in severe decline. AI researchers are throwing power at the problem. They're behaving like drunks at a free bar, as if there's limitless energy and they can consume as much as they want. AI is like one of those US gas-guzzler cars from the 1950s or 1960s, with not a care in the world for the world.

"In the AI field there is a dominant belief that 'bigger is better'," the AI Now Institute states. In other words, AI models that leverage processing-intensive mass computation are assumed to be "better" and more accurate. What they certainly are is much more expensive to feed.

Supposing we train AI to love energy like we love sugar? What sort of world would that create? AI's huge appetite for energy means that developments in the area are increasingly the domain of mega-corporations such as Google or Microsoft. The AI researchers in these behemoths don't notice because they have ready access to Herculean data centers. Academics, students and smaller companies notice though, as they find themselves increasingly being excluded from new developments because they can't bring enough power to the table.

There are much more energy-efficient approaches out there. Today, most computers are based on 64-bit processors. This sort of processing power is required for 3D graphics and virtual reality. However, much AI research and development can be done with 16-bit or 8-bit processors, Seokbum Ko, a professor at the University of Saskatchewan explains. A 64-bit processor consumes 64 times more energy than an 8-bit processor.

In digital, too few are asking the question: "How do we get the job done in the most environmentally friendly way with the minimum of energy?" We must change digital from a culture of waste to a culture of conservation. AI proponents love to talk about its benefits to the world, but they need to be much more aware of its costs to the environment.

The indirect pollution costs of AI may be even greater in that AI further encourages human convenience. Spotify has stated that people who listen to its service on smart speakers are more likely to listen to more music. All this music is stored in data centers and transferred across networks, all creating more pollution.

In the US, an individual smart speaker consumes between $1.50 and $4 of electricity per year. By 2021, it's estimated there will be 600 million smart speakers, generating at least one billion dollars annually of new electricity demand. If the smart speakers are linked up with a TV, for example, the TV's standby power consumption can increase by a factor of 20, adding an extra $200 of extra electricity costs over the lifetime of an average TV. Building up and maintaining the network that surrounds AI will be a highly energy-intensive enterprise.

When you ask Alexa to turn on the lights, "a vast matrix of capacities is invoked: interlaced chains of resource extraction, human labor and algorithmic processing across networks of mining, logistics, distribution, prediction and optimization," Kate Crawford and Vladan Joler write in Anatomy of an AI system. "The scale of this system is almost beyond human imagining." The scale of resources required is many magnitudes greater than the energy and labor it would take for us to get up off our bums and turn the bloody light off, not to mention the benefits of getting a bit of exercise.

As AI makes our lives simpler, easier and more convenient, we will likely become lazier, fatter and sicker. Researchers have found that app-based ridesharing resulted in the greater use of cars, and that e-scooters caused a reduction in people walking, cycling and using public transport.

Because an AI-controlled car may have 600-plus sensors, it will generate something like 6 GB of data every 30 seconds, Jack Stewart wrote for Wired in 2018. All this data needs to be processed in real time by a power-hungry decision engine. Then it needs to be stored and later analyzed. A typical driver uses their car for about one hour per day. For that hour, AI will generate 720 GB of data.

Let's say the car is used 250 days per year. (Based on our previous calculations, 100 GB of data creates about 0.42 kg of CO2, and a newly planted tree can absorb about 10 kg of CO2 per year.) What this means is that to deal with the yearly pollution that one AI-powered car emits, we'd need to plant 75 trees. It's estimated that there are over a billion cars in the world. If they were all AI-powered, we'd need to plant 75 billion trees, and that's just to deal with the pollution caused by data collection and transfer. We're currently planting about five billion trees a year.

Most AI cars will be electric. In 2018, about five million electric vehicles were sold globally, with sales doubling every year. One million electric cars will create about 250,000 metric tons of battery waste, which would be enough to fill almost 70 Olympic swimming pools.

"Our connectedness is using vast amounts of energy," science writer Angeli Mehta writes. The Internet of Things (IoT) promises to connect practically every object, system, animal and human into an almost unimaginable network of things. By 2025, there may be as many as 55 billion IoT devices. These billions of IoT devices will create zettabytes of data that will need to be transferred, stored and analyzed. The analysis will result in decisions that will need to be communicated back to the devices. All of this requires huge amounts of energy. If the data is used well, then the benefits of IoT in increased efficiency may outweigh its costs in energy consumption. May.

IoT devices require a lot of energy to manufacture because at the heart of IoT devices are logic circuits inside silicon chips. "The materials intensity of a microchip is orders of magnitude higher than that of 'traditional' goods," a paper from the United Nations University states. In other words, manufacturing IoT devices requires an order of magnitude more energy than manufacturing typical physical goods. These devices will have short lives, and when they are dumped, they will add another mountain range of e-waste to the many mountain ranges of toxic e-waste humans have created so quickly.

Bias inherent in history

"We are all in the gutter but some of us are looking at the stars," Oscar Wilde once wrote. Much of human history can feel like a gutter. It has been a long, hard struggle for human rights, for decency, for equality, for fairness. "Those who do not learn from history are doomed to repeat it" is reputed to be a quote from philosopher George Santayana. AI learns from history.

Smart speakers have the personas of coy female assistants because that's what the role of women was throughout history. Alexa, Cortana, Google Assistant, and Siri (which means "beautiful woman who leads you to victory" in Norse) represent not simply female assistants but "perfect" females. These assistants blush when they hear sexually explicit language, apologize that they are unable to make a sandwich, and generally behave like some men expect a nice woman should.

In an age when women and minorities are "misbehaving" and demanding fair treatment, AI is reinforcing stereotypes. AI is teaching kids and teens that the female AI assistant is there to serve their every whim, someone they can shout at and be abusive to. Thankfully, some of these bias issues are being recognized by designers and some good progress is being made. The challenge is not to teach AI history but rather to teach AI fairness.

An AI system was given 3.5 million books to analyze. Then it was asked its opinion of men and women. It described women as beautiful and sexy, while it described men as "righteous, rational, and courageous." An analysis of Google's job advertising system in 2015 found that men were far more likely to be shown ads for high-paid jobs than women were.

An Amazon job recruitment AI was almost exclusively selecting men because, well, the historical resume training data it was fed was almost exclusively male. Even though Amazon addressed some of the most blatant discriminatory issues, the AI was clever enough to find other ways to discriminate because that's the way it had been brought up—on lots and lots of manly data. That which you first feed AI shapes its character.

Historically, women who exhibit heart disease symptoms are "more likely to be diagnosed with anxiety and sent home, whereas if you're a man, you're more likely to be diagnosed with heart disease and receive lifesaving preventive treatment," Lisa Feldman Barrett writes in How Emotions Are Made.

The prejudices and sexism of male doctors throughout history has been used to train AI. When AI looks at medical research on heart disease it will find that the majority of the research is on men. So, it will "logically" assume that women don't get heart attacks. That's not true, of course. What is true is that the lives of women were not valued enough throughout history. AI systems diagnose women for anxiety when they should be diagnosing heart disease. The son is repeating the sins of the father.

Apple Card "is such a fucking sexist program," David Heinemeier Hansson wrote in 2019. "My wife and I filed joint tax returns, live in a community-property state, and have been married for a long time. Yet Apple's black box algorithm thinks I deserve 20x the credit limit she does. No appeals work." Nobody David talked to at Apple was able to help. Their constant reply was: "IT'S JUST THE ALGORITHM."

This reminds me of the text I used to see at the bottom of Google News: "The selection and placement of stories on this page were determined automatically by a computer program." Automatically? No possible bias so. It was all automatically done by a machine. Hey, if you think there might be some inherent bias in the news stories that we publish here at Google News, well, that couldn't be the case because the stories are chosen BY THE ALGORITHM and we all know that the algorithm is god.

Wherever there is bias in data, AI will pick it up and learn from it. AI will learn from poor quality data, from out-of-date data, from lies, half-truths, propaganda. AI will learn from whatever you feed it but what it learns may not be what you expect or want it to learn.

Amazon's facial recognition AI falsely identified one in six professional athletes from the Boston area, and one in five California lawmakers, as criminals. Amazon said that it was not the AI to blame but rather the people who were using it. Amazon claimed that the real purpose of its AI was to find missing children and stop human trafficking (cue violins). The gentle, caring folk at Amazon also said that seeing that the government was incompetent and didn't have a clue what was happening, maybe Amazon should be able to use an AI to write the laws that would govern the use of AI. (That's not a joke.)

Another AI system called COMPAS, when analyzing black and white people who had never been arrested, was twice as likely to label black people as high risk. Tay, a Microsoft AI chatbot, started off as a chirpy, fun-loving bot, and within 24 hours of interacting on the Web, had become a raving, foaming, Breitbart-spouting, Hitler-loving Nazi. AI learns super-quickly, you see.

Researchers who dug through nearly 50,000 records of a US hospital "discovered that an AI in use effectively low-balled the health needs of the hospital's black patients," Tom Simonite wrote for Wired. This wasn't a minor error. The AI system reduced the portion of black people who should have received help by 50%. This AI is believed to be used to manage the health of 70 million people in the US.

The algorithm wasn't even fed the race of the patients. It was clever enough to infer that from other information it was fed. It essentially learned from past inherent bias and prejudice in the data. In fact, the underlying bias was not so much about race but rather about being poor. The AI system chose to give rich people better care than poor people.

The United Nations special rapporteur Philip Alston has warned that with AI we risk "stumbling zombie-like into a digital welfare dystopia." In this dystopia, the rich become even richer and the poor get poorer and nothing can be questioned because IT'S THE ALGORITHM.

Sometimes AI, or what passes as AI, is just dumb—more like Artificial Ignorance. A manager at a large organization was hiring and was very disappointed by the quality of the people attending the interviews. By chance, she discovered that someone she knew who would have been perfect for the job had applied but had not been called for interview. She discovered that an AI system was being used to select interviewees based on a series of tests. The manager decided to take these tests herself and failed. She got other high-performing employees to take these tests and they practically all failed. And nobody in the company could explain how exactly the AI was deciding who should pass and who should fail. IT WAS THE ALGORITHM.

Dangerous mystery

How and why many AI systems make the decisions they make are a mystery, even to their creators. "Nobody understands THE ALGORITHM," David Heinemeier Hansson states. "Nobody has the power to examine or check THE ALGORITHM." We need transparent AI. We need to be able to hold AI to account. We need to be able to track back a decision, step by step. We need an understandable AI.

We most definitely need to build fairness into AI, establish for it a set of universal human rights, because "AI is expected to lead to increased economic inequality both across and within countries," the World Economic Forum stated in 2019. "Firstly, already-rich and technology-savvy countries are better prepared to leverage AI and harness its productivity gains... the rewards of AI accrue primarily to capital owners while the technology itself is largely labour-displacing. Most importantly, the jobs displaced by AI automation have distinct ethnic patterns."

Right now, AI is designed to pursue the Holy Grail of technologists down through the ages, which is the replacement of humans by technology. The deepest religion, the underlying philosophy, the culture of technology is that humans are the problem and that cost-cutting automation is the solution. There must be an algorithm that can do this better is how the minds of Mark Zuckerberg and Larry Page think.

Google did not start out as an idea for a search engine but rather as the dream of building the ultimate AI. Search data was to be used to train the AI, and how better to have an AI understand us than to have it learn from what we search for.

The potential of AI is immense, almost unimaginable. We must ensure an AI that is kind to the planet, that conserves energy rather than consuming it in increasing quantities as it currently does, that is fair and truly transparent so that we can understand it in the same way that it already understands us. To do that, we must nurture AI from its birth with an energy-efficiency mindset, feeding it quality, unbiased data, because what it learns first will establish the foundations of its DNA.

AI can save and take lives. In 2020, the BBC reported on a study conducted by Google Health and Imperial College London which created an AI that outperformed radiologists in reading mammograms to identify signs of cancer. On the other side, there is a debate about how much AI can be allowed to deal in death. "Twenty years from now we'll be looking at algorithms versus algorithms," Lt. Gen. Jack Shanahan, head of the Pentagon's AI initiative, told Wired in 2019.

"Unlike humans, AI is tireless," Fergus Walsh wrote for the BBC in 2020. As a glimpse of the future, in 2017 Facebook was forced to shut down an AI system that had developed its own language to communicate that the human developers could not understand. "It is as concerning as it is amazing—simultaneously a glimpse of both the awesome and horrifying potential of AI," Tony Bradley wrote for Forbes.

Supposing AI becomes like us? Supposing it has the same lack of respect for the Earth and other life on it? Supposing it becomes as addicted to energy as we are?

The future of AI is much too important to be left in the hands of technologists or militarists or any other single group. It is a matter than must concern everybody on this planet because before long it will affect the lives of everybody.

Key actions

Raise your voice about AI. Educate yourself about it. Talk to your friends; spread the word about its growing influence and power.

Demand that well-debated and well-thought-through laws are enacted to govern AI. Demand an ethical AI, an AI that always seeks to save energy rather than waste it.

Links

Cracking Ancient Codes: Cuneiform Writing, Irving Finkel, YouTube, 2019
https://www.youtube.com/watch?v=PfYYraMgiBA

The Evolution of Storage Devices, Rahul Chowdhury, HP, 2013
https://onextrapixel.com/a-look-into-the-evolution-of-storage-devices-1956-2013/

Sonos to deny software updates to owners of older equipment, Alex Hern, The Guardian, 2020
https://www.theguardian.com/technology/2020/jan/23/sonos-to-deny-software-updates-to-owners-of-older-equipment

Are Smart Speakers and Streaming Devices Energy Efficient? Noah Horowitz, NRDC, 2019
https://www.nrdc.org/experts/noah-horowitz/are-smart-speakers-or-streaming-devices-energy-efficient?

AI voice assistants reinforce harmful gender stereotypes, new UN report says, Nick Statt, The Verge, 2019
https://www.theverge.com/2019/5/21/18634322/amazon-alexa-apple-siri-female-voice-assistants-harmful-gender-stereotypes-new-study

Voice tech like Alexa and Siri hasn't found its true calling yet: Inside the voice assistant 'revolution', Rani Molla, Recode, 2018
https://www.vox.com/2018/11/12/17765390/voice-alexa-siri-assistant-amazon-echo-google-assistant

Green AI, R. Schwartz, J. Dodge, N. Smith, O. Etzioni, Allen Institute for AI, 2019
https://arxiv.org/pdf/1907.10597.pdf

Facebook AI Creates Its Own Language In Creepy Preview Of Our Potential Future, Tony Bradley, Forbes, 2017
https://www.forbes.com/sites/tonybradley/2017/07/31/facebook-ai-creates-its-own-language-in-creepy-preview-of-our-potential-future

At Tech's Leading Edge, Worry About a Concentration of Power, Steve Lohr, New York Times, 2019
https://www.nytimes.com/2019/09/26/technology/ai-computer-expense.html

The anatomy of AI, Kate Crawford, Vladan Joler, SHARE Lab, 2018
https://anatomyof.ai/

Can AI light the way to smarter energy use? Angeli Mehta, Ethical Corporation, 2019
http://www.ethicalcorp.com/can-ai-light-way-smarter-energy-use

Voice Recognition Still Has Significant Race and Gender Biases, Joan Palmiter Bajorek, Harvard Business Review, 2019
https://hbr.org/2019/05/voice-recognition-still-has-significant-race-and-gender-biases

I'd blush if I could: closing gender divides in digital skills through education, UNESCO, 2019
https://unesdoc.unesco.org/ark:/48223/pf0000367416.page=1

AI-powered automation will have an ethnic bias, Kai Chan, World Economic Forum, 2019
https://www.weforum.org/agenda/2019/07/job-losses-ai-automation

This machine read 3.5 million books then told us what it thought about men and women, Maria Hornbek, World Economic Forum, 2019
https://www.weforum.org/agenda/2019/09/men-women-books

Can you make AI fairer than a judge? Play our courtroom algorithm game, Karen Hao, Jonathan Stray, MIT Review, 2019
https://www.technologyreview.com/s/613508/ai-fairer-than-judge-criminal-risk-assessment-algorithm/

A Health Care Algorithm Offered Less Care to Black Patients, Tom Simonite, Wired, 2019
https://www.wired.com/story/how-algorithm-favored-whites-over-blacks-health-care/

AI's dirty secret: Energy-guzzling machines may fuel global warming, Donna Lu, New Scientist, 2019
https://www.newscientist.com/article/2205779-creating-an-ai-can-be-five-times-worse-for-the-planet-than-a-car/#ixzz5yHEiOwqf

Energy and Policy Considerations for Deep Learning in NLP, E. Strubell, A. Ganesh, A. McCallum, University of Massachusetts Amherst, 2019
https://arxiv.org/pdf/1906.02243.pdf

Intel Study: Applying Emerging Technology to Solve Environmental Challenges, Todd Brady, Intel, 2018
https://newsroom.intel.com/editorials/intel-study-applying-emerging-technology-solve-environmental-challenges/#gs.7lwnlh

How AI could save the environment, Alison DeNisco Rayome, Tech Republic, 2019
https://www.techrepublic.com/article/how-ai-could-save-the-environment/

Collaborative Intelligence: Humans and AI Are Joining Forces, H. James Wilson, Paul R. Daugherty, Harvard Business Review, 2018
https://hbr.org/2018/07/collaborative-intelligence-humans-and-ai-are-joining-forces

How AI can help us clean up our land, air, and water, Vox, 2018
https://www.recode.net/ad/18027288/ai-sustainability-environment

Self-driving cars could cause more pollution without dramatic changes to
the grid, P. Fox-Penner, J. Hatch, W. Gorman, GreenBiz, 2018
https://www.greenbiz.com/article/self-driving-cars-could-cause-more-
pollution-without-dramatic-changes-grid

Driverless Cars Generate Massive Amounts of Data. Are We Ready? Mark
Pastor, EnterpriseAI, 2018
https://www.enterpriseai.news/2018/10/24/driverless-cars-generate-
massive-amounts-of-data-are-we-ready/

Self-Driving Cars Use Crazy Amounts of Power, and It's Becoming a
Problem, Jack Stewart, Wired, 2018
https://www.wired.com/story/self-driving-cars-power-consumption-nvidia-
chip/

Intelligent Transportation Systems and Greenhouse Gas Reductions, M.
Barth, G. Wu, Kanok Boriboonsomsin, SpringerLink, 2015
https://link.springer.com/article/10.1007/s40518-015-0032-y

Artificial Intelligence—A Game Changer for Climate Change and the
Environment, Renee Cho, Columbia University, 2018
https://blogs.ei.columbia.edu/2018/06/05/artificial-intelligence-climate-
environment/

How artificial intelligence can tackle climate change, Jackie Snow, National
Geographic, 2019
https://www.nationalgeographic.com/environment/2019/07/artificial-
intelligence-climate-change/

AI and Climate Change: How they're connected, and what we can do about
it, AI Now Institute, Medium, 2019
https://medium.com/@AINowInstitute/ai-and-climate-change-how-theyre-
connected-and-what-we-can-do-about-it-6aa8d0f5b32c

Beyond the Smart Fridge: Leveraging the Internet of Things to Save the
World, Michael Wornow, Harvard Political Review, 2018
http://harvardpolitics.com/united-states/beyond-the-smart-fridge-
leveraging-the-internet-of-things-to-save-the-world/

AI 'outperforms' doctors diagnosing breast cancer, Fergus Walsh, BBC,
2020
https://www.bbc.com/news/health-50857759

ICT's potential to reduce greenhouse gas emissions in 2030, Jens
Malmodin, Pernilla Bergmark, Ericssson, 2015
https://www.ericsson.com/en/conference-papers/exploring-the-effects-of-
ict-solutions-on-ghg-emissions-in-2030

How to make computers faster and climate friendly, Seokbum Ko, University of Saskatchewan, 2018
https://theconversation.com/how-to-make-computers-faster-and-climate-friendly-101229

Twitter taught Microsoft's AI chatbot to be a racist asshole in less than a day, James Vincent, The Verge, 2016
https://www.theverge.com/2016/3/24/11297050/tay-microsoft-chatbot-racist

Amazon scraps secret AI recruiting tool that showed bias against women, Jeffrey Dastin, Reuters, 2018
https://www.reuters.com/article/us-amazon-com-jobs-automation-insight/amazon-scraps-secret-ai-recruiting-tool-that-showed-bias-against-women-idUSKCN1MK08G

Can the planet really afford the exorbitant power demands of machine learning? John Naughton, The Guardian, 2019
https://www.theguardian.com/commentisfree/2019/nov/16/can-planet-afford-exorbitant-power-demands-of-machine-learning

The Pentagon's AI Chief Prepares for Battle, Elias Groll, Wired, 2019
https://www.wired.com/story/pentagon-ai-chief-prepares-for-battle/

Cheap speed

Digital travels faster than physical. An email travels faster than a letter. A physical letter has constraints in relation to size, weight, cost. Digital communications costs seem vanishingly small. If I want to send a letter within Ireland it will cost me one euro for postage, and that does not include the cost of the paper or envelope. If I want to send an email anywhere in the world it costs me somewhere in the region of two hundred thousandths of a cent. Whereas a paper letter will take around 24 hours to arrive, my email will arrive in perhaps 24 seconds, certainly within 10 minutes.

When the cost is so small it's easy to think there's no cost at all. However, as we discovered earlier, to deal with email spam pollution, we'd need to plant 1.6 billion trees. To deal with legitimate email pollution, we'd need to plant 21 billion trees.

Speed and cheapness, what a powerful, intoxicating combination digital delivers. In the land of email, texting and Slack, things happen more quickly because they can. Those who take advantage of the speed opportunities can refashion industries. Fashion can be turned into Fast Fashion. The competitor who is not changing fast enough gets left behind. Fast Fashion may not be better fashion, but it is most definitely faster fashion, and when the price is so irresistibly low then the addictions blossom.

With digital, everyone is racing faster. To where? To the bottom, often. Factory workers get paid slave wages and fashion designers are being burnt out at a frenetic pace. Why? To dump a truckload of fashion every second?

Ah, but we humans, we can't resist speed, can we? I remember one dark, rainy winter night driving on a small Irish road. As I approached a bad bend, the signs kept warning me to slow down, slow down. Once I had gone around the bend and the straight road lay in front of me, there were no signs that encouraged me to speed up again. I did that naturally.

There are limits to speed though. The relationship of speed to risk is not dissimilar to the relationship of image resolution to image size. If you double the speed, you treble or more the risk.

An increase in average speed of 1 km an hour for a car increases the risk of a crash by 3%, with a 4–5% increase in the risk of a fatality. If you crash while driving at 80 km an hour, you are 20 times more likely to die than if you are travelling at 30 km an hour. There is also a link between speed and pollution. The harder the acceleration, the greater the spike in fuel consumption. Consistent, moderate speeds work best for the environment. Cheap thrills kill the environment.

Digital is an accelerant. Digital is fluid. In e-commerce, we used to be happy getting the delivery in a week, then it was a couple of days, then it was same-day delivery, and now the promise is one hour. Like with everything else, as speed increases so too do the risks and the costs.

If you're going to deliver very quickly then you will have to hold more stock, thus increasing costs and waste. The vehicles will be less efficient because they will tend to be partly loaded. Increasing speed of delivery is more stressful for the workers, with drivers having more accidents as they race to get something delivered on time. Amazon workers are set grueling targets, expected to scan items every 11 seconds, and measured and tracked with dystopian precision and ruthlessness. As a result, its US warehouse workers have twice the injury rate of the industry average.

When I was a teenager, I worked for a summer in Daimler Benz in Germany. My shift was from three in the afternoon until one in the morning. We had a quota to meet. However, most of us reached our quotas by eight or nine in the evening. We could go to the canteen, have a shower, do whatever we wanted. Germany was doing great. Workers were doing fine. They could have a good middle-class lifestyle. There was slack in the system, a bit of humanity, a bit of civilization.

What of today? What of progress? What of digital? Middle classes are shrinking, as some move up and more move down. To meet consumer desires for ever-faster deliveries, workers are exhausting and hurting themselves for minimum wages. That's not okay. That feels like digital is ripping up hundreds of years' worth of worker protection and rights, that digital is sending a large part of the workforce back to the nineteenth century. For what? So that Jeff Bezos, Mark Zuckerberg or Bill Gates can add another few billion to their pile of billions that they will never be able to spend?

It doesn't have to be this way. Digital doesn't have to be a wrecker of lives and destroyer of the planet. Properly used, digital can facilitate conservation. If that delivery truck is full and if it's going at a nice, consistent speed, and if the workers feel physically and mentally okay, then e-commerce can help reduce energy use, waste and pollution. If, on the other hand, speedy, frenetic e-commerce encourages the very worst frivolous, unnecessary purchases, then we'll all heading to hell in an Amazon package.

Links

Online shopping means cutting billions of trees, Akhileshwari Reddy,
DownToEarth, 2018
https://www.downtoearth.org.in/news/waste/online-shopping-means-
cutting-billions-of-trees-61296

What A Waste: Online Retail's Big Packaging Problem, Jon Bird, Forbes,
2018
https://www.forbes.com/sites/jonbird1/2018/07/29/what-a-waste-online-
retails-big-packaging-problem/#7d3a1019371d

Ruthless Quotas at Amazon Are Maiming Employees, Will Evans, The
Atlantic, 2019
https://www.theatlantic.com/technology/archive/2019/11/amazon-
warehouse-reports-show-worker-injuries/602530/

World Wide Worth

Worth

Think deeply about worth in your own context and in the context of the planet. Is it worth it? What are the implications of your decision for yourself next week, next month, next year? What are the implications of your decision on the planet next year, in the next ten years? What is the Earth Experience? Is it worth it?

- **Pay for value:** Pay for the stuff you value. Cheap takes from the future to serve the present. By paying for stuff, you will allow the people who make it to live off their work rather than to live off advertising. They will be better able to support the thing you value. They will be better able to improve it. If you don't value something then stop using it because chances are it's not that important to you. That'll give you more time to enjoy the things you do value.
- **Buy quality:** Buy stuff that lasts.
- **Create quality:** Create stuff that lasts.
- **Value yourself more:** Remember, if it's free, your personal data is the product, and the Earth is paying.
- **Keep it local:** The less distance stuff has to travel, the lesser the impact on the environment. For example, only save in the Cloud current stuff that's really important to you. For all the older and less important stuff, save to a local drive.
- **Avoid big brands:** The big brands are always multinational. They are always at a distance. We cannot make the world a better place without reducing the power and influence of the big brands.
- **Keep an eye on AI:** The worth of our world will be increasingly dictated by artificial intelligence unless we actively seek to ensure we get an ethical, environmentally friendly AI.

Waste

Stop the waste. Reduce the waste. Think about the waste. We don't have to sacrifice much of the good life that technology brings us. We must stop the waste, and by stopping the waste we will live better, more fulfilled, happier and healthier lives. And we'll save this precious planet so that our children and their children and all other teeming life can enjoy it.

- **Delete:** Think of your digital world as a nightclub that's full. You're the bouncer. To let something in, something else has to leave. When you take those 10 photos, delete eight. Don't let your digital garden get out of control. Weed every day. What are you going to remove today? Keep thinking about what you have, and whether you need it. Make review and delete part of your day.

- **Don't feed the ads:** Not reacting to the ads is one of the most powerful things you can do to reduce waste. Don't give your attention to the big brands.
- **Avoid packaging:** Eliminate as much packaging as possible because so much waste is packaging, and so much emotional marketing is packaging. A bar of soap is better than liquid soap in a plastic bottle.
- **Reuse:** Use the content or designs or code that others have created. Learn to love and admire old things. Wear your clothes until they're threadbare, then fix them or get them fixed. Use your products until they are truly worn, until the parts break. Then fix them or get them fixed or use them to create new products. (Create that circular economy.) Change equipment and software as rarely as possible. Hold on to things. Get maximum use out of stuff.
- **Share:** Share what you have as much as possible. If you're not using it, lend it or give it away.
- **Turn off:** When not using, shut down your computer, modem and other electrical appliances. Always optimize your use of energy. If you're going away, shut everything off bar your fridge and freezer.

Weight

Digital has a weight. Digital is getting heavier and harder for the planet to bear. We must measure it. We need to weigh the consequences of our decisions on the world not just on our world. Everything in digital is physical. Endeavor not too put on too much digital weight. Keep things light.

- **Lighter is better:** Start with the lightest option possible. Text is perfect. Less text is even more perfect. Only use images when they convey important information. Always optimize your images. Only use video when it is clearly the best option and keep it as short as possible.
- **Make digital weight visible:** The problem often is that digital is invisible. Make the weight of digital visible. Talk about it. Show it. Find clever way to make it visible so that people can "see" it.
- **Minimum data:** Stop tracking and collecting data unless there's an absolutely compelling reason to do so.

- **Minimum power:** Use the minimum power necessary to get the job done. Choose the minimum spec for the digital products you use.
- **Burn your own energy:** Get up and walk over to someone instead of sending that digital message. Burning your own energy reduces your weight and reduces the digital weight on the planet. Exercise more. Sweat more. Switch off technology. Plug it out for a while.

Wait

Too much speed kills the planet. Increasing speed has an exponential energy cost. Digital feeds the impulses. You must resist the instantaneous sense of convenience that digital offers. Rein in your gut instinct. Reasonable and consistent speeds are the most optimal and environmentally friendly approach.

- **Wait:** Learn to wait. Before you send that message, wait 30 seconds. Do you really need to send it? Do you really need to say "thanks" and send a big thread of correspondence back across the Web? Do you really need to use Google this time? Do you really need that ecommerce delivery so soon? Wait.
- **Slow down:** Break the digital habit. Resist the digital impulse. There can be so much joy is doing things slowly. Slow food. Slow fashion. Slow digital.
- **Think:** Use your brain more. Don't think twice, think ten times. Use your memory. Remember. Don't subcontract all your thinking to digital. Your mind is a wonderful place. Use it more.

Change is always possible

Montreal Protocol

The ozone layer protects our skin from many of the harmful elements of the sun's rays. Back in the 1980s, a huge hole in the ozone layer had opened up caused by the release of chlorofluorocarbons, chemicals widely used in refrigerators and air conditioners at that time. Chlorofluorocarbons are thousands of times more powerful than greenhouse gases such as carbon dioxide, and they stay in the atmosphere for hundreds of years.

The world came together and signed the Montreal Protocol which banned chlorofluorocarbons. The ban resulted in a phase-out of 99% of these ozone-depleting chemicals and the ozone layer has largely recovered. Humanity can work together and unified action works.

DNA does not have to be destiny. We do not have to be victims of our impulses. Digital has wonderful potential.

It's not enough for any one of us to individually change. Such incredible damage has been done to the Earth in the last forty years. We need radical steps to change a culture of overconsumption. We must come together in national and global movements because that is the only way we can change the system.

If you make the change to a less consuming life, try and get your friends and family to make the change too. Become political. Without a widespread political movement there is little hope of the systemic change we need.

3.5% change the world

3.5% of society changes society. This is the conclusion of research by Erica Chenoweth, a political scientist at Harvard University. She found that in society after society, organized non-violent disobedience by 3.5% of the population overturned dictatorships, forced governments to collapse, radically changed policies.

"Ordinary people, all the time, are engaging in pretty heroic activities that are actually changing the way [of] the world – and those deserve some notice and celebration as well," Erica Chenoweth stated.

The idea that we can't change anything, that our efforts mean nothing, is simply not true. If we organize and get close to a 3.5% movement, real and substantial change is more than possible.

Digital gives us tools of organization and networking that were historically the exclusive domain of the elites. It is no surprise that in the most repressive regimes, the first thing they do in a crisis is try and close down the Internet and the other communication networks.

We have so much organizing and communicating power at our fingertips. We must use it to good effect.

We are always changing

We think things don't change because we think short-term, we think in short spans of time. The further out we look the more change we see, and if we look far enough, we must surely look in wonder at the amazing adaptability of humans.

I grew up in a very small, rural community in county Longford, Ireland. As a child, one of my strongest memories was at funerals. There would be three or four shovels left at the graveside and once the priest had finished his prayers, the neighbors would start grabbing the shovels and shoveling the dirt onto the coffin. It was a sign of community and solidarity. However, to my child's eyes, it could sometimes feel a bit like a competition, as one man grabbed the shovel from another and busied himself shoveling as much clay as possible as quickly as possible.

I left that farming community and didn't return for many years. It was a funeral brought me back. I found myself waiting for that moment when I would now participate in this ancient custom. At the end of the prayers, instead of grabbing shovels, two men grabbed a cover of imitation grass and pulled it over the grave. I quietly asked my brother where were the shovels? He nodded towards a small mechanical digger.

We are always changing. Sometimes for the better. Sometimes for the worse. DNA is not destiny. We are coded to want more, to grab as much as possible because that's what was needed to survive for millions of years.

That which makes you strong can kill you in the end. We can and must adapt. We must retrain our gut instincts, learn that enough is enough, that less is nearly always better.

Links

The '3.5% rule': How a small minority can change the world
https://www.bbc.com/future/article/20190513-it-only-takes-35-of-people-to-change-the-world

Changing my behavior

It's hard to change my behavior. Hard to resist the call of new, of more. One thing I've tried is that whenever the urge to go to Twitter or Google News comes, I instead focus on reviewing and deleting. I've had some success.

We've done a lot of Top Tasks projects over the years where we help organizations identify what's most important to their customers. A core part of these projects is the running of surveys and the subsequent analysis. A lot of files are created in the process. When I examined the folder that contained the Top Tasks survey data I found that there were 12,861 files amounting to 13.9 GB of data. Did we need all these files and data?

To analyze the data, we created a plugin for Microsoft Excel. Thus, to process the data we needed a series of Excel files. For some reason, I can't remember why, we had also created an identical set of CSV files for every Excel file we created. I deleted them. There were unnecessary HTML files. I deleted those. There were copies, copies of copies, zip files, multiple versions of results, temp files. There was even a folder called "old files" with 1.60 GB of data in it. I deleted all these.

It was boring, repetitive work, though I didn't mind it. In a way, it felt meditative. It felt good. I was getting rid of useless waste, letting go stuff that was causing pollution and hurting the environment. At the end of the process, I had gone from 12,861 to 5,088 files, and from 13.9 GB to 1.07 GB. I had got rid of 92% of useless data, and I probably could have gotten rid of more had I worked harder. The Top Tasks folder is cleaner, easier to manage, and easier to understand.

I've been slowly reviewing the rest of my data world and there's so much junk, thousands of duplicate files, all sorts of crap. It's depressing. I've been such a participant at creating and storing gigabytes of crap.

I still waste time and the Earth's energy every day unnecessarily going online when I should instead be doing something physical or at least cleaning up a bit more of the digital poo I've left lying around.

There are small signs of progress. I'm working to get better, to downsize in all sorts of ways, to focus on what really matters and enjoy those things to the maximum. The light shines now and then and after maybe a period of cleaning up some digital junk, and some extra focus on the important stuff, there is a quiet sense of satisfaction.

It's a work in progress.